This book
belongs to

.... Bella Mackenzie

Children's
PICTURE
BIBLE

Retold by
Carol Watson

Illustrated by
Lucy Su and Mary Lonsdale

zigzag

For Abraham Shehadi

Author

Carol Watson has written over fifty books for children, including Bible stories and two books of children's prayers. After seven years of teaching she worked for a number of international publishers before becoming a freelance writer.

Consultant

Revd Richard Adfield PG Dip Coun trained as a Church of England minister at Oak Hill College in London. For many years, he was a vicar in London when he specialised in children's talks. He is now a hospital chaplain and counsellor.

8082
This edition published in 1998 by Zigzag Publishing.
Copyright © 1995 Zigzag Publishing, a division of Quadrillion
Publishing Ltd, Godalming, Surrey, GU7 1XW.

Edited by Philippa Moyle
Designed by Patrick Knowles
Cover illustration by Lucy Su
Cover design by Kate Buxton

Colour separations by Master Image, Singapore
and RCS Graphics, Leeds, England.
Printed in Hong Kong

A CIP catalogue for this book is available from the British Library

ISBN 1-85833-883-2

Contents for the Old Testament

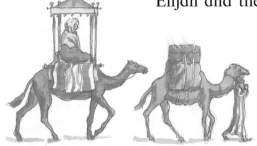

Contents for the New Testament

Introduction

Did you know that the Bible is not *one* book, but a huge collection of books that have been put together? These include history, poetry, letters and true stories of people's lives. The books are divided into two main sections – the Old Testament and the New Testament.

If you read the whole Bible from beginning to end you can discover what God is like, and find out about his love for his creation – the world and its people. The Bible tells how, over thousands of years, God keeps faithful to those who believe and trust in him. It also contains God's laws which tell us how to behave if we want to live at peace with him and each other.

This *Children's Picture Bible* contains some of the most important and exciting stories from that large collection of books. As you read about the many different characters and their adventures and friendships, you will see how much God helps and strengthens those that turn to him.

The Old Testament is about God's relationship with the Jewish people over hundreds of years. It tells of their wanderings and struggles, and of the many leaders God chose to help them. The New Testament tells about God's own son, Jesus. God loves us so much that he sent his only son into the world to give *all* people a chance of a relationship with him.

Carol Watson

The Old Testament

The word *testament* means an agreement or promise. The Old Testament tells the story of God's promise to Abraham and his descendants, the Jewish people. This promise was that if they obeyed and trusted in him, and kept his laws, he would always love and protect them. Even when his people disobeyed his rules, God showed that he was a loving Father by giving them more and more chances to change their ways and turn back to him.

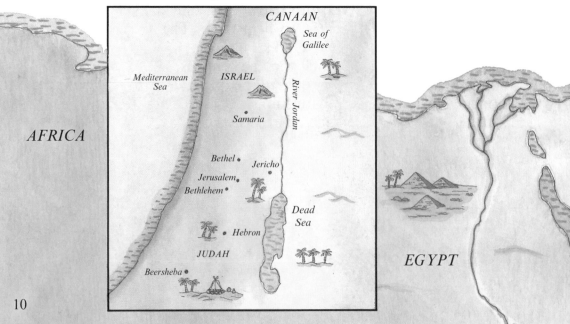

10

Black Sea

MESOPOTAMIA

Haran

Ninevah

River Euphrates

River Tigris

SYRIA

Mediterranean Sea

Babylon

CANAAN

Jericho
Jerusalem

Ur

SINAI

ARABIAN
DESERT

Red Sea

The Creation Story

Long ago, before the world began, there was darkness everywhere. So God decided to make light to shine into the darkness. He called the light 'day' and the darkness he called 'night'. This was the first day.

Then God parted the seas and made dry land appear. On this empty and lifeless land God created beautiful green trees and plants with colourful flowers and luscious fruit. He filled the fruit with seeds so that more plants and trees could grow.

God was pleased with his world, so he went on to make two lights in the sky, called the sun and the moon. These were to separate day from night and to act as signs to mark the seasons, days and years. God made the sun to shine brightly during the day and he made the moon and stars to give out a gentler light at night.

"Now I shall fill my world with living creatures," thought God. He made birds to fly in the sky, fish to swim in the seas, and all kinds of animals, both great and small, to roam on the land. He told the creatures to have young and multiply so that they would spread over all the earth. God was happy with everything that he had made. So, he decided to make people to enjoy his creation, and to take care of it.

First, God created a man called Adam. He put Adam amongst the beautiful trees and plants of the Garden of Eden. Then, to keep Adam company, God made a woman, called Eve. Adam and Eve lived happily in the Garden of Eden and God provided everything they needed.

In the middle of the garden were two special trees. One was called the Tree of Life. The other was called the Tree of the Knowledge of Good and Evil. God told Adam, "You may eat from any tree in the garden, but you must not eat from the Tree of the Knowledge of Good and Evil, for if you do you will surely die."

The enemy of God, the Devil, decided to make Adam and Eve disobey God's command. He used a crafty snake to persuade Eve to eat from the forbidden tree. The snake told her that if she did this she would become as wise as God.

So, Eve ate from the tree and tempted Adam to eat, too. As soon as they had disobeyed God and eaten, Adam and Eve knew right from wrong, and they were ashamed. God was very angry. He cursed the snake and banished Adam and Eve from the Garden of Eden. Because they could no longer reach the Tree of Life, Adam and Eve could not eat its fruit and live for ever.

"From now on, you will have to work hard for what you need to live," said God.

Adam and Eve had chosen to disobey God. Now they had to make their own way in the world.

Cain and Abel

After Adam and Eve had left the Garden of Eden, Eve had two sons, called Cain and Abel. The elder son, Cain, became a farmer and his brother, Abel, was a shepherd.

One day, the two sons decided to make offerings to God. Cain brought the best corn from his crops, and Abel's gift was a newborn lamb from his flocks. God looked at Cain and Abel. He knew what sort of people they were. God saw that Abel had a warm, loving heart, but he also saw that Cain was cold, selfish and proud.

So, God accepted Abel's offering, but he did not want his brother's gift at all. Cain was furious with God and he became sullen and moody. When God saw this he spoke to Cain. "Cain, why are you so angry?" asked God. "If you do what is right I will accept your present, but you must overcome your bad thoughts and feelings."

Cain did not want to hear what God was telling him. He was hurt and angry, and jealous of his brother, Abel.

Some time later, Cain asked Abel to go for a
walk in the fields with him. Abel was pleased
and happy that, at last, he and his brother
could be friends again. As they strolled along,
Cain looked at Abel's smiling face. Suddenly he
was filled with a great hatred and jealousy. Cain
turned on his brother and, with one almighty
blow, knocked him down and killed him. Then,
terrified by what he had done, Cain ran away.

However, God knew what had happened.
Again He spoke to Cain. "Cain, where is your
brother, Abel?" God asked.

"I don't know," Cain replied. "Do you expect
me to look after my brother all the time?"

God said, "Cain, what have you done? You
have killed Abel, your own brother. Your
punishment will be very great." Then God told
Cain, "From now on, the earth will no longer
give you fine crops to eat, and you will be
forced to travel the world as a homeless
wanderer."

Cain cried out in despair, "My punishment is
more than I can stand. How can I live like that?
Whoever I meet will know what I have done
and they will kill me."

God promised Cain that he would protect him,
and that he would live unharmed. So, Cain
left his farm and moved away. Because he
had chosen to hate his brother instead of
to love him, Cain had also moved away
from God in his heart.

Noah's Ark

The murder of Abel by his brother, Cain, was the first wicked thing to happen in the world. Although the people on earth now knew the difference between good and evil, as time went by, many chose to disobey God and live wicked lives. God was hurt and angry at the way people behaved. He began to regret that he had created people at all. Finally, he decided to destroy everyone in a great flood.

There was, however, one man who had pleased God. His name was Noah. So, God warned Noah about what was coming and told him to build a huge boat. "I am going to put an end to people, because the earth is filled with violence," said God. "I am going to destroy all life under the heavens in a flood. But, I promise that you and your family will be saved."

God told Noah exactly what shape and size to build the large wooden ark in which his family would escape the floods. Noah was to coat it inside and out with tar to make it waterproof. Then God said, "You are to take into the ark two of every living creature, male and female, to keep them alive with you," said God. "Also take with you food of every kind for your family and the animals."

So, Noah did everything that God had told him. Then he and his sons, Shem, Ham and Japheth, took their wives on to the ark.

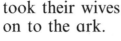

The Flood

One week after the people and animals were safely aboard the ark, the first drop of rain splashed down. Then it rained and rained. It rained for forty days and forty nights, until the rivers and seas rose and flooded the land. Soon, even the tops of the mountains had disappeared and every other creature in the world had drowned. Noah and his family floated safely in the ark on a deep and endless ocean.

After many weeks, the rain stopped. God sent a strong wind to blow and, gradually, the waters began to go down. One hundred and fifty days later, the water level had sunk so much that the ark came to rest on the mountains of Ararat. But Noah and his family still did not dare leave it. Six weeks later, Noah opened a tiny window in the ark and sent out a raven. It just flew around in circles waiting for the tree tops to appear. Then Noah sent out a dove to see if the water had gone from the surface of the ground. But the dove could find nowhere to settle, so it returned to the ark.

A week later, Noah once again let the dove fly away. This time she flew back with an olive leaf in her beak. Now Noah knew that there was something alive and growing in the world. After another week had gone by, the dove went on her third flight. She did not return, so Noah knew she had found somewhere to live.

Then Noah and his family removed the huge roof covering the ark and saw that the surface of the ground was dry. God said to Noah, "Come out of the ark. Your family is safe. Bring the animals out and let them go free to roam the earth and multiply."

Noah and his family were very happy to be out of the huge boat and back on land again. They made an altar and offered gifts to God to thank him for sparing their lives. God was pleased with Noah and blessed him and his sons. "Go and have many children," said God. "Spread out and fill the earth. I give you charge of everything that is in the world. All that lives and moves will be food for you."

God promised Noah that he would never again send a flood to destroy the earth. He called this promise his covenant. "I have put a rainbow in the sky," said God, "and it will be a sign to remind you that I will always keep my covenant with you and everything on the earth that lives."

So, after that time people in the world knew that if it rained they should not be afraid. Whenever the sun shone through the clouds a rainbow appeared, and then everyone remembered God's promise to Noah.

The Tower of Babel

After the flood, Noah's sons, Shem, Ham and Japheth, took their families and settled in different parts of the land. From them grew many nations of people. Although these people were scattered over the world, at this time everyone spoke the same language and could understand each other's speech.

One group of people travelled east until they came to a grassy plain. As the land was flat, they settled there and decided to build themselves a great city. "Let's make a tower that is the highest in the world," they said. "It will be so tall that it will reach up to the heavens. Then our city will be famous throughout the land."

So, they set to work. Instead of using stone they baked their own bricks, and instead of using mortar they stuck the bricks together with tar. The tower grew taller and taller, and the citizens were very pleased with their creation.

However, God saw what was happening and he was sad. Once again, the people on earth were becoming selfish. They were not interested in loving and helping each other, but were competing with each other to be the most important. God decided to act before things got any worse.

"If people speaking one language can plan to become so powerful," thought God, "then it is time to confuse them, so they do not understand one another."

Suddenly, everyone in the city began to speak in different languages. There was pandemonium and the building of the tower stopped. The people left the city and, together with all their strange languages, were scattered to the far corners of the earth.

After that the abandoned tower was known as Babel, because God made a babble of the language of the world.

21

The Adventures of Abraham

For many years after the Tower of Babel, God watched the people of the world closely. He was trying to spot another fine and honest man like Noah. God needed someone who loved and trusted him so much that he would obey all his commands. This person was to be chosen by God to start a new and special nation. Finally, God found someone.

One of the descendants of Noah was a man called Terah. He lived with his family in Mesopotamia. The story of the nation of Israel begins with his son, Abraham.

As an old man, Terah set out with his family to travel from the city of Ur to the land of Canaan. On this long journey he stopped at a place called Haran, and decided to settle there instead. Terah stayed in Haran until he died.

Then God spoke to Abraham, "Leave your country, your people and your father's household and go to the land of Canaan." Abraham was amazed. He was by now quite an old man, with many possessions and huge flocks and herds. At his age, it was difficult to leave everyone and everything he knew to travel to another land.

But Abraham was, above all things, obedient to God. So he took his wife, Sarah, his nephew, Lot, and all their flocks, herds and possessions and set off for the land of Canaan.

On the way, Abraham stopped at different resting places. Each time, he built altars to God and prayed. God told Abraham that he was going to give this land to Abraham's children.

After a time, the flocks of Abraham and Lot grew so large that there was not enough pasture land for them all to stay together. Abraham said to Lot, "Let's not have any quarrelling between you and me, or between your herdsmen and mine. Choose where you want to be and I will go elsewhere."

So, Lot chose to go to the rich pastures of the Jordan valley, and Abraham stayed in the hill country in Canaan.

Then God spoke again to Abraham. "Don't worry," he said, "I am going to keep you from harm and give you everything you could ever want." But Abraham was sad. He did not really want riches and land and great possessions. All he wanted was a child. Now he and Sarah were too old to have a baby. "Lord, what pleasure can I get from anything," said Abraham, "as long as I am childless? I have no heir, and when I die my servant will inherit all I possess."

Then God told Abraham that his servant would not be his heir. "Your descendants will be as numerous as the stars in the sky," said God. "Your wife, Sarah, will have a son, and you must call him Isaac." Abraham was puzzled but he knew he could trust God.

Isaac is born

After a while, God blessed Sarah just as he had promised. She became pregnant and gave birth to a son. As God had commanded, his parents called him Isaac. Abraham and Sarah were overjoyed with their little baby, and he was more precious to them than anything else in the world.

Some years later, when Isaac had grown into a fine boy, God decided once again to test Abraham's obedience. He asked Abraham to take Isaac to a deserted place and offer him as a sacrifice. Abraham must have been horrified at what he had to do. How could he kill his beloved son? But he knew he must obey God in all things. So, with a heavy heart, he set out with Isaac to go up into the mountains, to the place of sacrifice.

On the way, Isaac said to Abraham, "Father, we have wood for the fire and the knife to kill the animal, but we have no lamb for the burnt offering."

Abraham answered, "God will provide the lamb for the sacrifice, my son." And so they travelled on.

When they reached the place God had told them about, Abraham built an altar and arranged the wood on it. Then he tied up his son, Isaac, and laid him on the altar on top of the wood. Just as Abraham raised the knife to kill his son, God called out.

"Abraham! Abraham!"

"Yes, Lord," Abraham replied.

"Do not lay a hand on the boy," said God. "Do not harm him in any way. I know now that you obey me in all things. You love me so much you were prepared to sacrifice your precious only son."

Abraham looked up. He saw a ram caught by its horns in a bush. So, instead of his son, Abraham made the ram his sacrifice to God. And God blessed Abraham and told him that his descendants would be as numerous as the grains of sand on the seashore.

"Through your offspring all the nations on the earth will be blessed," said God, "because you have obeyed me."

Then, Abraham and Isaac made their way back down the mountain and went home.

Isaac and Rebekah

Time went by, and Isaac grew up into a handsome, young man. Abraham was now very old and, before he died, he wanted to make sure Isaac married a loving wife from his homeland.

So, Abraham sent for his chief servant and said to him, "I want you to promise by the Lord, God of heaven, that you will not find a wife for my son from the land of Canaan, where we now live. Promise you will go back to my own country to find a wife for Isaac."

"But, what if the woman doesn't want to come and live in Canaan with us?" asked his servant. "Shall I then take your son back to the country you came from?"

Abraham told his servant that Isaac must stay in Canaan. "The Lord promised me that he would give this land to my offspring," said Abraham. "God will guide you to the right girl."

So, the servant took ten camels laden with presents, and set off for Mesopotamia, the land Abraham had left behind many years before. At last he came to the town of Nahor, and took his camels to rest at the well.

It was evening, and the time when the women of the town went to the well to collect water for their families. Then the servant prayed to God.

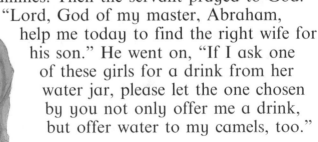

"Lord, God of my master, Abraham, help me today to find the right wife for his son." He went on, "If I ask one of these girls for a drink from her water jar, please let the one chosen by you not only offer me a drink, but offer water to my camels, too."

Abraham's servant had hardly finished praying when a beautiful, young girl came to the well, carrying a water jar. Her name was Rebekah, and she was a distant relation of Abraham. Rebekah went to the well and filled her jar.

"May I have a little water from your jar?" asked the servant.

"Please drink, my lord," said Rebekah, and she lowered her jar and offered him some water. Then Rebekah said, "Let me give your camels a drink, too." And she ran back to the well to collect more water for Abraham's camels.

When the camels had finished drinking, the servant gave Rebekah presents of gold jewellery and asked her about her family. When he heard that Rebekah was a relation of Abraham, he thanked God for guiding him to the right place.

Rebekah's brother, Laban, greeted the visitor and welcomed him to their home. That night, before they ate supper, Abraham's servant told the family why he had come to that place, and all about the prayer he had prayed at the well.

Everyone agreed that it was God's will that Rebekah should be Isaac's wife, and Rebekah, too, was willing to go to Canaan. So Rebekah returned with the servant and she and Isaac were married. They loved each other and lived happily together.

Esau and Jacob

Isaac and Rebekah had twin sons, called Esau and Jacob. Esau grew up to be a big, bearded, hairy man, who loved the countryside and was skilled at hunting. He was his father's favourite, and Isaac liked to eat the wild game caught by his strong son. Jacob, on the other hand, was a quiet, thoughtful sort of person. He was much more business-like than Esau, and preferred to be at home. Jacob was his mother's favourite.

Before the twins were born, Rebekah had been told by God that, when they grew up, the older child would serve the younger. She had found this puzzling, but always kept it in her mind. Esau was the elder of the twins as he had been born first. So, he was due to receive the birthright from their father, Isaac. This meant that Esau would be head of the family after his father's death. Also, with the birthright, Esau would receive Isaac's blessing for the future. Rebekah could not see how God's prophecy could come true.

Jacob, however, was jealous of Esau and tried to think of a way to trick him. One evening, Esau returned home exhausted by a day's hunting. He felt very hungry, and there was a delicious smell wafting through the air. Esau rushed in to find Jacob cooking a stew.

"Quickly, give me some meat," he said to Jacob, "I'm starving!"

Jacob stared at Esau and thought for a moment. Then slowly he replied, "If you give me your birthright, I'll give you some stew."

Esau was only interested in eating. "What good is my birthright to me when I'm dying of hunger," he replied. "Let me eat!"

"Promise me first," said Jacob. So, Esau swore an oath to Jacob, promising to hand over his birthright. Jacob gave him the food and Esau ate greedily. Rebekah had seen everything and she did not forget it. How little Esau had valued his birthright, to sell it for a plateful of stew!

Many years went by, and Isaac grew old, frail and blind. It was time to give his blessing to his eldest son. So, Isaac told Esau to go off and hunt some wild game for him to eat. "Prepare me the kind of tasty food I like and bring it to me," he said, "so that I may give you my blessing before I die."

Rebekah overheard Isaac talking to Esau. Instead of leaving things to God, she decided to act while she could. Rebekah told Jacob what had been said. "Now, my son, listen to me," she said. "Go out to the flock and bring two young goats, so that I can prepare a tasty stew. Then you can take it to your father, and he will bless you before he dies."

"But my brother, Esau, is a hairy man," said Jacob. "What happens if my father touches me? He would know I was tricking him, and he would curse me instead." Rebekah told Jacob to leave everything to her. So he went off and brought the goats to his mother, and she prepared the stew.

Jacob tricks Esau

When Rebekah had cooked the stew, she dressed Jacob in Esau's clothes, and covered his hands and the smooth part of his neck with goatskins. Jacob took the tasty food and went into his father's tent.

"My father," said Jacob.

"Yes, my son," answered Isaac. "Who is it?"

"I am Esau, your firstborn," lied Jacob. "I have done as you told me and brought you the game, so that you may give me your blessing."

Isaac was not sure that it was Esau, so he asked Jacob to come close so that he could touch him. Isaac felt Jacob's hands and neck, and they were hairy like those of Esau. But it seemed like the voice of Jacob. "Are you really my son, Esau?" Isaac asked.

"Yes," replied Jacob. "I am."

After he had eaten, Isaac asked Jacob to kiss him. As he came close, Isaac could smell Esau's clothes and then he truly believed that it was his eldest son. So, Isaac gave his blessing to Jacob. "May God give you everything. Be lord over your brothers, and may the sons of your mother bow down to you. May those who curse you be cursed and those who bless you be blessed."

After Isaac had blessed him, Jacob left his father. He had only just gone when Esau returned from hunting. He, too, prepared his father's favourite food, and took it in to Isaac.

Then poor old Isaac knew that he had been deceived and told Esau what had just taken place. When Esau heard that Jacob had tricked him and received the blessing he cried bitterly over what he had lost. He swore to kill Jacob once Isaac was dead.

When Rebekah heard that Esau was planning revenge, she warned Jacob. "You must leave at once," she said. "Go and stay with my brother, Laban, until Esau has calmed down. I'll send for you when the time is right."

Then Rebekah told Isaac that she wanted Jacob to marry a woman from their homeland, just as Isaac had done. Isaac agreed and sent for Jacob. "You must not marry a Canaanite woman," he told Jacob. "Take a wife from the daughters of Laban, your uncle. May God bless you and your descendants as he did Abraham, so that you may take possession of Canaan, as was promised."

So Jacob set off for Mesopotamia, the land of his forefathers, to escape his brother's anger and to find himself a wife.

Jacob's Ladder

Jacob travelled alone on the long journey to his uncle's house, so he had plenty of time to think about what he had done. He turned things over in his mind and wondered what the future would hold for him now. It grew dark, so Jacob decided to stop for the night. He took a large, smooth boulder to use as a pillow, and lay down on the ground to sleep.

As Jacob slept he had a strange dream. He dreamt he saw a large stairway leading from earth to heaven and, moving gently up and down it, were the angels of God. Then Jacob heard the voice of God speaking to him. "I am the Lord, God of Abraham and Isaac," he said. "I will give the ground on which you are lying to you and your descendants. They will spread all over the world and people on earth will be blessed through you and your children. I will watch over you, wherever you go."

When Jacob woke up he remembered his dream vividly. "This is a holy place," he thought. "I feel God's presence here." So, Jacob took the boulder he had used as a pillow, and stood it upright like a pillar. He made it an altar to God and called the place Bethel, which means 'house of God'.

Then Jacob knelt down and prayed. "Lord, if you will take care of me until I return safely to my father, then I will serve you faithfully."

Feeling strengthened, Jacob continued on his journey. At last he arrived at Haran where Laban, his uncle, lived. Jacob stopped to drink at a well, and there he met some shepherds who knew his relations. "Here comes Laban's daughter, Rachel, now," they said. "She's bringing her father's sheep to the well."

Jacob helped Rachel to water his uncle's sheep. When she discovered who he was, she ran quickly and brought her father. "Welcome, Jacob," cried Laban, "how good it is to meet my sister's son!" Laban hugged and kissed his nephew, and took Jacob to live in his home.

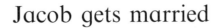

Jacob gets married

Jacob worked hard for Laban, helping with his flocks and herds. After a month had gone by, Laban said, "Just because you are my nephew doesn't mean you should work for no wages. What payment do you think is fair?" Jacob thought for a moment. Laban had two daughters, Rachel and Leah. Rachel, the younger of the two, was very beautiful. "I'll work for you for seven years," he said, "if you let me marry your daughter, Rachel." Laban agreed.

Seven years later, the time came for Jacob to marry Rachel. Laban arranged a great wedding feast and that night gave Jacob his bride. But it was not Rachel that Jacob had married. Hidden under the veil was her sister, Leah. Now Jacob knew what it was like to be tricked. He was furious. But Laban said, "It is not our custom here to give the younger daughter in marriage before the older one. You can marry Rachel, too, if you work for another seven years."

Jacob loved Rachel so much that he worked for his uncle for seven years more. During this time, Laban's flocks grew very large. God was watching over Jacob, so he was successful in everything he did. At the end of seven years Jacob married Rachel.

Jacob's first wife, Leah, had six sons and a daughter, but for a long time Rachel did not have a child. Leah was jealous of Rachel because Jacob loved her, but Rachel envied Leah because of her children. At last, God blessed Rachel and she, too, had a baby boy called Joseph.

As Jacob was so hard-working, Laban wanted
him to stay always in Haran. But one night,
after Joseph had been born, God told Jacob
it was time to return to Canaan. So, Jacob
gathered his families and flocks and, while
Laban was away, secretly set out for the land
God had promised to give his descendants.

On the journey back, Jacob thought again
about Esau. He prayed to God to protect him
from his brother's anger. That night he sent
his family and flocks to camp ahead of him,
and stayed on his own to pray. He hoped God
would speak to him and guide him.

For a while nothing happened. Then someone
seemed to appear out of the darkness and press
against Jacob. He pushed them away but the
person just forced him back. Soon Jacob was
wrestling with the unknown visitor in a terrible
struggle. They wrestled together all night long
until, as dawn was breaking, the stranger
touched Jacob's hip. He shrieked in pain as the
bone went out of joint. Then a voice said,
"Jacob, you have struggled with man and God,
and you have won your battle to survive. From
now on you will no longer be called Jacob, but
your name will be Israel, and your descendants
will be called Israelites."

Then the stranger disappeared and the pain
went from Jacob's hip. Jacob wondered if he
had been dreaming again, but when he stood up
he discovered he had a limp. Then Jacob knew
that he had been wrestling with God.

Joseph and his Brothers

When Jacob finally met Esau again, his brother had forgiven him and greeted Jacob with affection. So, Jacob and his family returned safely to live in Canaan.

By now, Jacob had twelve sons and one daughter. Out of all his sons, Rachel's firstborn, Joseph, was Jacob's favourite. To show how much he loved Joseph, Jacob gave him a special, long-sleeved coat of many colours. In those days, it was a great privilege to own such a coat, and Joseph's brothers were jealous of Jacob's love for him.

One night, Joseph had a strange dream. The following day, he told his brothers about it. "I dreamed we were all out in the fields harvesting the sheaves of corn," said Joseph. "Suddenly, my sheaf stood upright, and all your sheaves made a circle round mine and bowed down to it."

Not surprisingly, the brothers were angry. "Who do you think you are, that we should bow down to you?" they shouted. Not long afterwards, Joseph had another dream. He told the family about it. "I dreamed that the Sun and Moon and eleven stars were bowing down to me," said Joseph.

Even Jacob was irritated. "Do you think you are going to be more important than your mother, brothers and me?" he asked. By this time, Joseph's brothers hated him so much that they began to plot against him.

One day, Jacob sent Joseph off to the fields to check that his brothers and the sheep were safe. When his older brothers saw him approaching, they said, "Here comes the dreamer. Let's kill him now, and then we can tell Jacob that a wild animal has eaten him. That will put an end to his dreams!"

However, Reuben, the eldest son, said, "We must not harm him. Let's just throw him into this pit and teach him a lesson." So, as Joseph drew near, the brothers tore off his fine coat, and threw him into a dried-up well. Then Reuben went to check the flocks and the others sat down to eat.

As the brothers were eating, a group of Ishmaelite traders came along. "Let's sell Joseph to these foreigners," said one brother. "Then we will be rid of him for ever!" So, for twenty pieces of silver, they sold Joseph to the Ishmaelites.

When Reuben returned he was horrified, and wept for Joseph. But the others tore Joseph's coloured coat and dipped it in goat's blood. Then they returned home to Jacob and said sadly, "We found this coat. Surely it belongs to our brother, Joseph?"

Jacob immediately recognised the blood-stained coat of his favourite son and cried out, "My precious son, Joseph, is dead. A wild animal must have killed him!"

Poor Jacob. No one could comfort him.

Joseph and Pharaoh's Dreams

Joseph was taken to Egypt where he was sold as a slave to a man called Potiphar. He was Captain of the Guard to Pharaoh, the king of Egypt.

Joseph worked hard for Potiphar, who put him in charge of the whole household. However, Potiphar's wife had fallen in love with Joseph. She began to pester him to return her love, but Joseph was too honest to take advantage of her. "How could I betray my master's trust?" Joseph said to himself. "Besides, it is a sin against God."

When she couldn't get her own way, Potiphar's wife was angry. So, she pretended that Joseph had attacked her, and Potiphar ordered Joseph to be thrown into the royal prison. There he remained for many years.

While he was there, Pharaoh's butler and baker were brought to the prison for displeasing their master. One morning, the two prisoners looked miserable. "We both had strange dreams last night," they told Joseph, "and we don't understand what they mean."

God helped Joseph to understand the meaning of the dreams. "In three days' time you will be given your job back," he told the butler. Then he turned to the baker and said, "I'm sorry, but in three days' time you will be taken out and hanged from a tree." It was Pharaoh's birthday three days later. He ordered the chief baker to be put to death, and gave the butler his job back.

Two years later, Pharaoh had two vivid dreams which none of his wise men could explain. The butler remembered Joseph and brought him before the king. "The God whom I worship helps me to understand the meaning of dreams," Joseph told the Pharaoh.

So, Pharaoh told Joseph his dreams. "I saw seven fat cows come out of the river to feed on the grass. Then seven thin, bony cows came along and ate up the fat ones." Pharaoh went on. "In my second dream, I saw seven ripe ears of wheat growing on one stalk. Then seven thin, withered ears of wheat sprouted and swallowed up the ripe ears."

Joseph explained that God was preparing Pharaoh for the future. Both dreams meant that there were going to be seven years of good crops followed by seven years of famine.

Pharaoh was impressed by Joseph. "God has given you great wisdom. I will make you governor of all Egypt."

Joseph ordered huge storehouses to be built in every city. During the next seven years, there were wonderful harvests. Vast amounts of wheat were stored away. Then came the bad years. Joseph organised the distribution of the stored wheat, and foreigners came to Egypt to buy some at a high price.

The Famine in Canaan

The famine spread to Canaan where Joseph's family lived. Jacob and his sons needed food. "There is grain for sale in Egypt," said Jacob to his sons. "Go there and buy as much as possible, so that our family will not starve."

The brothers set off for Egypt. All, that is, except Benjamin, as Jacob could not bear to be parted from his youngest son.

When they finally came before him, Joseph recognised his brothers immediately. But they, of course, had no idea who he was. His brothers did not expect to see Joseph ever again, and certainly not dressed as an Egyptian.

Joseph pretended not to believe who they were. He accused them of being spies and kept them in prison for three days. Joseph said he would only believe they were not spies if they returned with their youngest brother who, they had told him, remained at home in Canaan.

Keeping one of the brothers hostage, Joseph sent the rest to Canaan to fetch Benjamin. He sold them sacks of grain to take with them, and commanded his servants to put the money paid for the grain secretly into the sacks.

When they opened the sacks, the brothers were terrified. "Now we will be accused of being thieves as well as spies!" they said. However, they returned safely to Canaan, and provided food for the children of Israel.

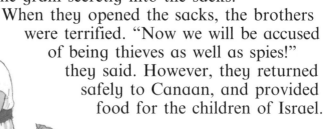

After a while, the grain ran out and Jacob told his sons that they must return to Egypt, or they would starve. "But, Father, we cannot go back there unless we take Benjamin with us," said the brothers. "Otherwise we will all be arrested as spies." Eventually, Jacob reluctantly agreed to let Benjamin go.

Joseph was delighted to see Benjamin again. He released his other brother from prison, and invited them all to have dinner with him. The brothers still did not recognise Joseph.

When it was time for them to leave, Joseph secretly ordered his servants to put the money the brothers had paid for the grain into the sacks. "Also," he said, "hide my silver cup in the sack of Benjamin, the youngest." His servant did this.

As the brothers were travelling back to Canaan, Egyptian horsemen thundered towards them. Joseph's steward searched the sacks. When he reached Benjamin's sack, he pulled the silver cup out of the grain. "We have been tricked!" cried the brothers. But the soldiers arrested them, and they were marched back to Egypt, trembling with fear.

Jacob travels to Egypt

Joseph summoned his brothers, who bowed low before him. "Benjamin, who stole the cup will remain here as my slave," said Joseph. "The rest of you may go free."

Joseph had put his brothers in this position to discover just what sort of men they were. So, he was pleased and moved when Judah stepped forward and said, "If you keep Benjamin here, our father will die of grief. Please let me stay in his place."

With tears in his eyes, Joseph dismissed his servants from the room. Then, speaking in Hebrew for the first time, he said, "I am Joseph, your brother! Do you not know me? See, my dreams have come true and you have all bowed down before me."

His brothers were terrified when they realised that this was their father's favourite whom they had sold into slavery. However, Joseph forgave them and hugged and kissed them all. "It was all meant to happen this way. God planned for me to be here, so that his people would not starve."

Joseph told them about the years of famine yet to come. "Return to Canaan and tell Jacob that God has made me governor of all Egypt. Bring our father, and your wives and children. Come and live here as richly as I do."

Joseph's brothers brought their old father, Jacob, and all their families out of the famine in Canaan, and so it was that the children of Israel settled in the land of Egypt.

The Birth of Moses

After four hundred years, the children of Israel had grown into a large nation and lived in a part of Egypt called Goshen. The Pharaoh at that time feared that the Israelites would become too powerful, so he treated them harshly and forced them to work as slaves.

Despite their cruel treatment, however, the Israelites still thrived and grew in numbers. So, Pharaoh decided to take drastic action. "Every baby boy born to the Israelites is to be drowned in the River Nile," he ordered his soldiers.

And that is exactly what happened. The poor Israelite women wept and wailed as their little sons were brutally killed. But one of them, a woman called Jochebed, hid her baby boy.

After three months, it became impossible to keep the boy a secret. So, Jochebed had an idea. She found a small basket and coated it with pitch and tar to make it waterproof. Then she wrapped her baby warmly and put him inside. Jochebed carefully placed the basket to float amongst the tall reeds at the edge of the river, and her daughter, Miriam, hid close by to watch what happened to the little child.

Soon afterwards, Pharaoh's daughter came to bathe in the cool water. As she wandered along the riverbank, she saw the basket amongst the reeds, and ordered her slave girl to fetch it.

"It's a baby!" cried Pharaoh's daughter, as she looked inside. "It must be one of the Israelite boys." The child began to cry and the princess felt sorry for him. "Poor little thing," she said, "he wants his mother. I shall look after this baby, and care for him as my own son."

When Miriam heard what was said, she went over to the princess. "Shall I find an Israelite woman to nurse the baby for you?" she asked.

"Yes, go," said Pharaoh's daughter. So, Miriam went to find Jochebed.

"Take this baby and nurse him for me," the princess told Jochebed, "and I will pay you." Jochebed was delighted. Now she could care for her own baby boy without being afraid. When he was older, Jochebed took her child to the palace and Pharaoh's daughter brought him up as her own son. She named the boy Moses.

God calls Moses

As he grew up in Pharaoh's palace, Moses was given the best of everything. He was taught to read and write, dressed in fine clothes, and rode around in a chariot. But, although Moses appeared in every way to be an Egyptian, he never forgot that he was really an Israelite.

Moses saw how badly the Egyptians treated his people. He was angry, and wanted to help them. One day, he saw an Egyptian viciously beating an Israelite slave. He could stand it no longer, and in his anger he killed the Egyptian. Before long, the news of this murder reached Pharaoh, and he ordered Moses to be put to death. So, Moses fled from Egypt.

Moses travelled into desert regions, stopping at a place called Midian. He worked there as a shepherd to a man called Jethro. Moses married one of Jethro's daughters and they had a son.

One day, Moses was tending the sheep in a deserted place near the mountains of Sinai. Suddenly, he saw flames leaping from a bush. Moses went nearer to put out the fire but, although the bush appeared to be alight, the flames were not harming it at all.

"That's strange," thought Moses, and he watched carefully.

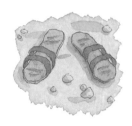

Then he heard a voice calling, "Moses, Moses, do not come any closer. Take off your shoes, for this is holy ground." Moses knew that this was the voice of God. He waited in awe to hear what was said.

"I am the God of your father, the God of Abraham, the God of Isaac and the God of Jacob," said God. "I have seen the suffering of my people in Egypt, and have heard their prayers. It is time to rescue them from the Egyptians, and to give them the Promised Land of Canaan. I want you to go to Egypt and lead my people out of slavery."

Moses was terrified when he heard this, and begged God to send someone else. But God told Moses that all his enemies in Egypt were now dead, and there was nothing to fear. The Lord said, "I will be with you, and when you have brought the people out of Egypt, you will worship me on this mountain."

"What if they don't believe me or listen to me?" asked Moses.

God told Moses that he would do many miracles and great wonders to prove to his people, and to the Egyptians, that he was the one true God. As Moses had a slight stammer, God said he could take his brother, Aaron, with him to do the talking. God said, "Take the staff that is in your hand, so that you can perform great wonders with it."

So, Moses was obedient to God. He took his wife and children and, with the wooden staff in his hand, he set off back to the land of Egypt.

Moses and Pharaoh

Meanwhile, in Egypt, God also spoke to Aaron, so he went off to find his brother, Moses. When the two men met, Moses told Aaron all that God had instructed him to do.

Then Moses and Aaron travelled together to Egypt, and met with the elders of the Israelites. They performed miracles and great wonders, so that the Israelites truly believed that Moses was sent by God to help them.

Now it was time to tackle Pharaoh. Moses and Aaron requested an audience with the Egyptian king. When, at last, they stood before Pharaoh they announced, "The Lord God of Israel says, 'Let my people go, so that they may worship me in the desert.'"

But Pharaoh replied, "I do not know your Lord and I will certainly not let the Israelites go."

So, Moses and Aaron went on, "The God of Israel has asked us to go into the desert to offer him sacrifices. If we do not obey, God may strike Egypt with plagues."

But Pharaoh lost his temper, and told Moses and Aaron to get back to work. He was so furious, he made life even harder for the Israelite slaves, and they were beaten all the more.

So, the elders of Israel came to Moses and complained bitterly. "You have just made matters worse," they said. Moses knew they were right and he felt dismayed and confused.

But God spoke to Moses again. "Do not be afraid," he said, "you will soon see what happens to Egypt. I will make Pharaoh so sorry that he will almost beg the children of Israel to leave." And God again promised Moses that his chosen people, the Israelites, would go free.

So, Aaron and Moses asked to see Pharaoh once more. They warned him that if he did not let the people of Israel go free, God would bring terrible disasters upon his country.

But Pharaoh just laughed. "The Israelites will not leave," he said. "I do not believe in your God." And he sent Moses and Aaron away.

So, God did as he had promised. Soon strange and terrible things began to happen in Egypt.

The Nine Plagues

First, God told Moses to take his staff and touch the surface of the River Nile. As he did so, the water turned red as blood and all the fish in the river died. There was not a drop of water in Egypt that anyone could drink.

Next, God sent a plague of frogs upon the land. Thousands of large, slimy frogs teemed out of the stinking river water and filled the palace and houses. They hopped around the kitchens, jumped on the food and slithered inside the beds of the Egyptian people.

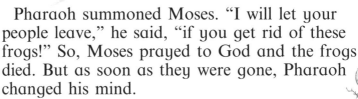

Pharaoh summoned Moses. "I will let your people leave," he said, "if you get rid of these frogs!" So, Moses prayed to God and the frogs died. But as soon as they were gone, Pharaoh changed his mind.

Then God sent a plague of thousands of stinging gnats, followed by millions of huge, fat flies which swarmed into every house and covered the ground in a great crawling mass. So, once more, Pharaoh promised to let the Israelites go, but again he changed his mind.

After that, God killed all the Egyptian sheep, goats and camels, and plagued the Egyptian people with huge, festering boils. Still Pharaoh would not budge.

So, the Lord sent a terrifying storm over
Egypt. Lightning flashed to the ground, thunder
roared and huge hailstones pelted down,
crushing everything beneath them. But Pharaoh
would not free his slaves.

Then God sent a plague of hungry locusts
which flew in dense black clouds and devoured
all the crops. There was nothing green left on
any tree or plant in all the land of Egypt.

When Pharaoh still remained stubborn, God
brought a terrible darkness over the Egyptians.
For three days, it was so black that no one
could see anything at all.

Throughout these plagues, Goshen, the area
where the Israelites lived, did not suffer many
of the awful plagues sent to the Egyptians.
God was showing the king of Egypt who was
in control.

But even after all that had happened, Pharaoh
still refused to let the children of Israel leave
Egypt. "Get out of my sight!" he screamed at
Moses. "If I see you again you will die."
So, Moses left Pharaoh and waited
to see what God had planned next.

The First Passover

God had planned a disaster for Egypt that was more terrible than anything that had ever happened before.

The Lord said to Moses and Aaron, "On the night that I tell you, each Israelite family is to kill a lamb and smear its blood on the doorframe of their house. Then, dressed ready to leave, they must eat the lamb, roasted with bitter herbs."

Then God told them, "On that same night the Angel of Death will pass through Egypt and strike down every firstborn male child and animal. But when I see a door marked with blood I will know that those people worship me. The Angel of Death will pass over that house, and no harm will come to those who live there."

God told Moses that, from then on, they were to remember that day and make it a time of celebration. "When your children ask you what this celebration means, tell them, 'It is the Passover sacrifice to the Lord, who passed over the Israelite homes when he struck down the people of Egypt.' "

So, Moses and Aaron told the children of Israel what God had instructed them to do.

At midnight, on the day chosen by God, the eldest son of every Egyptian family was struck dead. From Pharaoh's palace to the poorest hovel, there was not an Egyptian home in which someone had not died. Never had there been such weeping and wailing throughout the land.

During that same night, Pharaoh summoned Moses and Aaron. "Go! Leave my people, you and your Israelites," he cried. "Get out of here. Worship the Lord as you wish. And take your flocks and your herds with you."

The Egyptian people were so afraid of any further disaster, they urged the Israelites to go quickly. They gave them gold and silver jewellery, and fine clothing to take with them.

As there was no time to wait for their bread to rise, the Israelite women took the dough they had prepared, wrapped it in cloth, and carried it with their possessions as they fled.

And so, that night, hundreds of thousands of Israelites, men, women and children, left Egypt with their flocks and herds. After their many years of slavery, at last they were free.

Crossing the Red Sea

Moses led the Israelites into the desert, and they began their journey to the Promised Land of Canaan. As Moses did not know which way to travel, God guided the children of Israel with a pillar of cloud during the day and a pillar of fire at night. They came, at last, to the shores of the Red Sea, and set up camp as God had commanded them.

Meanwhile, yet again, Pharaoh had changed his mind. After the Israelites had gone, the Egyptian king realised just how many slaves he had lost. So, Pharaoh gathered his huge, powerful army, and set out to capture the Israelites and bring them back to Egypt.

The children of Israel saw Pharaoh's army approaching, and found themselves trapped between the Egyptians and the sea. The people were terrified and shouted at Moses, "Have you brought us out of Egypt to die in the desert? We would have been better off as slaves!"

But God had spoken to Moses, and he calmed the people. "Do not be afraid," he said to them. "God will keep you safe. He will fight for you. This is the last time we will be troubled by these Egyptians."

Moses stretched out his staff over the sea in front of them. As he did so, God sent a great wind which divided the waves, making a pathway through the water. So, the Israelites began to cross over to the other side.

But the Egyptians chased after them across the sea-bed. Just as the Israelites reached safe ground, God let the vast walls of sea-water pour back down again, and the mighty army of Egypt was drowned beneath the rushing waves. The people of Israel thanked God for saving them. Now they were able to begin their long journey through the desert.

In the Desert

For the next three days, the Israelites travelled through the hot desert without finding water. At last, they saw ahead of them a large pool. But when the Israelites drank the water, it tasted bitter, so they still could not quench their terrible thirst.

The people grumbled at Moses. "What are we supposed to drink?" they asked. And again they began to wish they were back in Egypt. So, Moses prayed to God, and the Lord guided him to a piece of wood nearby. Moses threw the wood into the pool and the water became sweet. So, the Israelites were able to drink from the pool and refresh themselves for their long journey.

But, after a while, the food ran out. And again the Israelites moaned. "At least when we were in Egypt we had plenty to eat," they said to Moses. "Have you brought us into the desert to starve?"

So, God told Moses that he would provide the Israelites with meat to eat in the evening, and that in the morning they would find as much bread as they could possibly want.

That same night a flock of quail flew down from the sky. The Israelites caught some of the birds and had a fine meal of roast meat.

Then, the next morning, there was a heavy layer of dew around the camp. When the dew had gone, thick, frost-like flakes appeared on the ground. Moses told the people to collect this and eat it. It tasted like wafers made with honey. "What is it?" they asked.

Moses told them it was the bread that God had provided for them. "Each morning you are to gather what you need for the day," said Moses. "On the sixth day you must collect enough for the seventh day which is the Sabbath. God orders you to rest on the seventh day." The Israelites called the food 'manna'.

And so, the children of Israel trekked on. But as they grew short of water once more, the people soon forgot all that God had done for them. They began to complain again. In fact, they were so angry with Moses that he began to fear for his life.

God said to Moses, "Take the elders of the Israelites and go on ahead of the people. I will guide you to a rock. Strike it with your staff, just as you did the River Nile."

So, Moses did this. As his staff touched the rock, water gushed out and the Israelites were able to drink their fill.

Moses hoped that at last the children of Israel would stop doubting God's plan for them, and learn to trust him more.

The Ten Commandments

Three months after the children of Israel had left Egypt, they reached Mount Sinai where God had first spoken to Moses. They set up camp in the desert below the great mountain.

Moses went up the mountainside to be quiet and to pray to God. As he prayed, God told him that, in order to show the Israelites that Moses was their chosen leader, God was going to speak to Moses in front of them all. "I am going to come to you in a thick cloud," said God. "The people will hear me speaking to you and put their trust in you."

God told Moses that the Israelites were to prepare themselves to come before God. They were to wash their bodies and their clothes, and make themselves pure in every way. Then they were to come to the foot of the mountain, but to go no further. So, Moses instructed the Israelites to do all that God had told him. Then he made a boundary line round the foot of the mountain, which the people were not to cross.

Three days later, there was terrible thunder and lightning, and a fire on the mountain caused billowing smoke to form a large, dense cloud. The whole mountain shook violently, and a sound of trumpets pierced the air. The children of Israel were terrified.

Then Moses went up the mountain to listen to the Lord. God gave Moses ten commandments, or laws, to tell his chosen people. These were rules about the correct way to behave. If the people obeyed these rules, they would live happily and peacefully together and with God, but if they disobeyed the rules their relationship with God and each other would be difficult.

God told Moses, "You must not worship any other gods instead of me." He did not want his people to make anything or anybody more important in their lives than him. He told them not to worship other idols, or to use his name as a swear-word. "Remember to keep the Sabbath day special," said God. The Lord wanted those who believed in him to set aside the seventh day of the week to rest and worship him. It was to be a holy day, or holiday.

God went on to say that everyone should respect and honour their parents, and children should do what their mother and father thought best for them. God told Moses that those who believed in him should not murder, steal or lie. They should not desire something that belonged to someone else, and those who were married should remain faithful to each other.

Then God engraved the ten laws on two large, flat stones, called tablets, and he told Moses that all those who obeyed the laws and worshipped him would be blessed.

The Golden Calf

After God had given Moses the laws for his people, he spoke to Moses again. God renewed his promise to give the land of Canaan to the children of Israel, just as he had promised Abraham many years ago. But God told Moses he would only keep this promise if his chosen people obeyed the laws he had given them.

To remind the children of Israel that he was always with them, the Lord told Moses to construct a large tent, called the tabernacle. Inside this, the Israelites were to place a wooden chest, called the ark. God told Moses to put into the ark the ten commandments that he had given to his people. This meant that wherever they travelled, and whenever they set up camp, the Israelites carried the law with them. The tabernacle was to be the holy place of God and the ark was the most sacred thing of all.

Moses spent many weeks listening to God on the mountain. He was away from the camp for such a long time that the Israelites grew impatient and began to doubt Moses would return. The people even began to doubt God's existence at all. They gathered round Aaron and bullied him, saying, "Moses has disappeared, and we don't know what has happened to him. Give us gods that we can worship now."

So, Aaron asked for their gold jewellery, which he melted down and made into a large golden calf. Then they made sacrifices to the calf and had a great feast.

God saw the Israelites feasting. "Already my people disobey me," he said angrily. Moses hurried down to the camp, carrying with him the tablets of stone. As he saw the people singing and dancing round a golden idol, he was filled with rage. He hurled down the stone tablets and smashed them on the ground. Then he ground the golden calf into powder, mixed it with water and made the people drink it. After that, Moses went back up the mountain to beg God's forgiveness for what they had done.

God was very angry with the Israelites, and Moses had to plead with him not to abandon his chosen people. Finally, God agreed that he would still lead the children of Israel into the Promised Land.

So, Moses wrote God's commands on new tablets of stone and took them back down the mountain to the crowds waiting below. "You must now obey these laws and make a fresh start," Moses said to the people, "or the Lord will abandon you for ever."

The Israelites were very relieved when they saw Moses return, his face shining with joy. They were sorry for what they had done and agreed to obey God's laws.

And so they continued on their journey to the land of Canaan. But it was to take a lot longer than they thought!

The Promised Land in Sight

At last, the children of Israel drew near to Canaan. They were very excited as, it seemed, their travels were nearly at an end. Moses assembled the people and said, "Get ready, we are going to take this land that God has promised us. Don't be afraid. The Lord is with us." But the Israelites were nervous. They asked Moses to send men ahead to spy out the land. So Moses agreed, and sent twelve spies to see what they could find.

After a few weeks, the spies returned. They brought back luscious fruit to show the Israelites and had much to tell about the places they had seen. "It's a wonderful country," they said. "Just look at the fruit that grows there." They went on, "But the people are very powerful, and their huge cities will be difficult to attack."

Two of the spies, Caleb and Joshua, were keen to go in and take the land. "We can do anything with God's help," they said.

But the others were gloomy and afraid. "We can't overpower those people. They are as big and as strong as giants!" The other ten spies spread terrifying stories around the camp.

That night, the children of Israel moaned and wailed at Moses. "We should never have left Egypt," they said. "We want another leader instead of you."

Joshua and Caleb urged the people to trust in God and to go into Canaan. But the Israelites grew so angry that they picked up stones to hurl at the two spies.

Suddenly, a great light appeared above the tabernacle of God, and the Lord spoke to Moses. "Enough! I have brought these people out of slavery, given them everything they need and performed great miracles, and still they cannot believe in me." God continued, "These people will never enter the land of Canaan. They will wander in the desert for another forty years. I will give the Promised Land to their children, and the two faithful spies, Caleb and Joshua, will lead them."

So, because of their disobedience and lack of faith, the children of Israel were forced to return to the desert for the next forty years. All this time, despite everything they did to anger him, Moses remained their faithful leader. He was a very old man when, finally, the time came for the Israelites to enter the Promised Land.

But God had told Moses that he would not go into Canaan. "Climb to the top of Mount Pisgah," said God. "While you are looking out at the Promised Land, your life will come to an end."

Before Moses left the Israelites, he again told them to obey God's laws. Then he turned to his friend, Joshua. "Be strong and courageous," he said. "You are to lead the people now."

Then Moses slowly climbed up to the top of the mountain and looked out at the beautiful country of Canaan stretched before him. He had obeyed God and his job was over. There, on the mountainside, the great prophet died.

Joshua enters Canaan

After Moses had died, the Lord spoke to Joshua. "Moses, my servant, is dead," he said. "I want you to lead these people across the River Jordan and into the Promised Land of Canaan. As I was with Moses, so I shall always be with you. I will never leave you as long as you obey my law. Be strong, confident and determined to win."

So, Joshua called the elders of the Israelites. "Tell the people to get ready," he said. "In three days' time we are going to cross the river and enter the Promised Land."

The first city across the border was Jericho. This was surrounded by tall, thick walls, and seemed impossible to capture. So, Joshua sent two men to spy on the city. While they were there, the spies came to the house of a woman called Rahab.

The king of Jericho heard about the spies and sent his soldiers to search them out. But Rahab believed that God was going to give Jericho to the Israelites, so she hid the spies from the king's soldiers on the roof of her house. In return for their safety, Rahab asked for the safety of her own family when the Israelites did take control.

"Gather all your relatives into the house with you," said the spies, as they escaped from her house down the city walls. "And keep this red rope hanging from your window as a sign. Then, when the city falls, no harm will come to those that live here."

The spies returned to Joshua and reported what had happened. Now it was time to cross the river.

Joshua told the people to prepare themselves, as God was going to do amazing things. Then he appointed twelve priests to carry the ark of God to the edge of the River Jordan. The people were to follow a little way behind.

"You will know today that the Lord is with you," Joshua said to the children of Israel. "When the priests carrying the ark of God set foot in the Jordan, the waters of the river will stop flowing and stand up in a great wall. Then all Israel will cross to the other side."

And it all happened as Joshua had told them. Many thousands of Israelites walked across the river bed. And, just as had happened in the Red Sea, once they were safe, the water flowed back again. After that, the children of Israel knew that God was with Joshua and they obeyed him in all things.

The next problem was Jericho. As they drew near to the city, Joshua wondered about the battle plan. So, God sent an angel to tell Joshua what to do. The instructions seemed a little odd, but the new leader realised that they must be obeyed.

The Fall of Jericho

Joshua gathered the Israelites and told them God's plan. "Seven priests carrying trumpets are to walk in front of priests carrying the ark of the Lord," said Joshua. "An armed guard will go ahead of the ark, and a rear guard will march behind. They will march silently round the city once a day, for six days. Then, on the seventh day, the priests will blow their trumpets, and everyone will march around the city seven times. When the priests blow a long blast on their trumpets, everyone is to shout as loudly as they can."

So, the Israelites did as they were instructed. Inside the walls of the city, the people of Jericho peered out at the strange goings on. As each day went by, they grew more and more afraid. Then, on the seventh day, there was an incredible din. The Israelite army was shouting, and the sound of trumpets pierced the air.

Suddenly, there was a terrible rumbling sound, and the walls of the city started to tremble and shake. Then, with a strange groaning noise, the mighty walls of Jericho fell crashing to the ground. The Israelite army marched in and captured the city with ease.

Throughout it all, Rahab and her family were safe. Rahab survived because she had believed and trusted in God.

Gideon and the Midianites

Joshua led the children of Israel on to many successful battle campaigns throughout Canaan, and the land that was captured was divided between the twelve tribes of Israel. But this was just the beginning of the conquest of the Promised Land. There were still areas that the Israelites did not control.

For many years after the death of Joshua, the children of Israel had no strong leader. They disobeyed God's laws and worshipped false gods. As a result, they lost God's protection and came under the rule of several powerful enemies.

The Midianites were a fierce desert people who terrorized the children of Israel for years, raiding their crops and carrying off all their animals. A young Israelite, called Gideon, was determined to outwit them. He grew his wheat in secret and threshed it in a winepress to keep it hidden.

One day, Gideon was feeling very downhearted about the Midianites when he heard a voice saying, "You are not alone. God is with you, mighty warrior." It was an angel of God, and he had come to tell Gideon to lead the Israelites against their enemy. Gideon was terrified. He wondered how he could achieve this impossible mission. But God answered, "I will be with you, and you will wipe out the Midianites with one blow." And the Lord told Gideon to start by pulling down the huge statue of Baal, the god which the enemy worshipped. So, Gideon did this, and set up an altar to the Lord in its place.

Then Gideon took as many soldiers as he could muster into the mountains overlooking the vast army of the Midianites. God said to Gideon, "Announce to your soldiers, 'Anyone who is afraid of battle may leave now.'" Thousands of Israelite soldiers fled. Finally, with only three hundred soldiers at his side Gideon prepared to attack.

Gideon divided his soldiers into three groups, and they spread around the Midianite camp. Each man carried an earthenware jar, a torch of oiled wood and a trumpet made from a ram's horn. "Watch me," Gideon told his men. "When I get to the edge of the camp do exactly as I do."

In the middle of the night, and hiding the flames of their torches inside the jars, Gideon led his men towards the enemy camp. Then, as Gideon signalled, the Israelite soldiers blew their trumpets and smashed the earthenware jars. "A sword for the Lord and for Gideon," they shouted, waving their flaming torches in the air.

The sleeping Midianites woke up to find themselves surrounded by light and noise. They thought a huge army had come against them. In their panic, they turned and fought against each other. Then, thinking that all was lost, they took to their heels and ran away. As promised, God had given Gideon a great victory, and he had not even drawn his sword.

Because Gideon had obeyed God, the Israelites lived in peace for the next forty years.

Samson is born

During their time of peace, the Israelites again began to forget God's laws, so new enemies rose up against them. One of the most powerful of these enemies was the Philistines, who ruled over the Israelites for forty years. The Israelites who were faithful to God prayed for a new leader to deliver them from the Philistines.

Manoah and his wife were an Israelite couple who had been childless for many years. One day, an angel of God appeared to Manoah's wife and said, "You are going to have a baby boy. Do not drink any alcohol and be careful what you eat. The boy must be dedicated to God as a Nazarite, so the hair on his head must never be cut. He will be the one who starts to help Israel defeat the Philistines."

After the angel had gone, the woman ran to tell her husband what had happened. Manoah was amazed and prayed that the angel would come to him to repeat God's message. So, the angel appeared to Manoah and told him that his wife must do as God had instructed her. The couple were overjoyed that, at last, they would have a child. They made an altar to the Lord, and offered up a sacrifice of thanks. Some time later, Manoah's wife gave birth to a fine boy, and she named him Samson.

As the angel had said, Samson was brought up as a Nazarite. This meant that he belonged to a special group of Israelites set aside for God, who never cut their hair or drank alcohol. Samson grew up to be a big, handsome man, with long flowing hair and incredible strength. His parents doted on their only child, and Samson was used to having his own way.

One day, Samson announced to his parents that he was getting married. At first, they were pleased, but then they discovered that his future bride was a Philistine girl. As usual, Samson got his way and, reluctantly, his parents agreed to the marriage. So, the three set off on the journey to meet the bride's family. While Samson's parents were walking ahead of him, a lion sprang out to attack Samson. With his amazing strength, Samson fought the lion and killed it with his bare hands. Then he ran to join his parents.

Some time later, when he travelled the same route to the marriage ceremony, Samson saw the carcass of the lion he had killed. In it there was a swarm of bees and some honey. Samson scooped up the honey and ate it on his journey.

Samson's Wedding

Samson's wedding went ahead, and at the marriage feast there was much merrymaking. "Let me tell you a riddle," Samson said to the thirty Philistine men who were gathered at the party. He bet the men thirty suits of clothing that they wouldn't discover the answer to his riddle before the end of the week. This is what he told them:

"Out of the eater came something to eat.

Out of the strong came something sweet."

The men racked their brains but they couldn't think of the answer to the riddle. They were so irritated with Samson that they persuaded his new bride to coax the answer out of her husband. Then they answered Samson:

"What is sweeter than honey?

What is stronger than a lion?"

When Samson heard this, he knew that his wife had betrayed his trust. He flew into such a rage that he went out and killed thirty Philistine men, and gave the dead men's suits to those who had explained the riddle. Then, furious with his new wife, he left her and went back to his parents, swearing to take revenge on the Philistine nation.

After this, there was much more violence and hatred between Samson and the Philistines. And Samson began a campaign against them, killing many of his enemy and hiding away in a cave.

Eventually, the Philistines were so enraged by Samson that they invaded the area where he lived. The Israelites of Judah were horrified at what Samson had brought upon them, and went to find him in his cave.

To save Israel from further trouble, Samson agreed to be tied with thick ropes and handed over to the enemy by his fellow Judaeans. The Philistines were delighted. At last, they had Samson, but not for long! With his strength, Samson heaved on the ropes that bound him and snapped them in two. Then, grabbing the jawbone of a donkey which was lying nearby, he hacked his way through the thousand Philistine men who had come to take him away.

After that, Samson led Israel against the Philistines for twenty years. Throughout all this time, his enemy looked for a way to overcome Samson's superhuman strength.

Eventually, an opportunity arose. Samson fell in love with another Philistine woman. Her name was Delilah, and she was very beautiful. Little did Samson know that the woman he loved was paid by his enemy to trap him.

One night, as she lovingly stroked his hair, Delilah asked Samson, "Tell me the secret of your great strength and how it would be possible to overpower you."

Samson finally told Delilah the truth. "No razor has ever been used on my head," he said, "because I have been a Nazarite since the day I was born. If my head were shaved then my strength would leave me."

So, Delilah secretly drugged Samson's drink to make him sleep. While he slept, Delilah's servant shaved Samson's head and his strength left him. Samson awoke to find himself surrounded by Philistine soldiers. He jumped up to fight them, but found he was too weak. Then he knew he had been tricked.

Samson in the Temple

The Philistines blinded Samson, bound him with chains, and took him away to prison. There he remained for many months, and during this time his hair grew again.

So overjoyed were they with the capture of Samson, the Philistines organised a great celebration. Thousands of them flocked to the temple to rejoice and worship their god, Dagon.

As they crowded into the huge building, the people roared loudly, "Bring out Samson to entertain us!"

Samson was led out of prison to perform in front of his enemies. As he stood there, blind and in chains, the hordes of Philistines jeered and mocked him. But Samson stood erect, with his head held high. He turned to the servant who led him and said, "Lead me to the two pillars in the centre of the temple, so that I can lean against them."

Standing between the two central pillars, Samson prayed to God. "Please strengthen me once more," he said. "Let me, with one blow, get revenge on these people." And Samson reached out to touch the pillars on which the whole temple rested. He braced himself and cried out, "Let me die with the Philistines!" Then Samson pushed and heaved with all his might, and the huge pillars cracked and split. Suddenly, with a noise like thunder, the vast temple came crashing down.

As he died, Samson killed more Philistines than in all the years that he had lived.

The Story of Ruth

The period of time when Gideon, Samson and others led the Israelites against their enemies was called the time of Judges. These were people that God raised up to lead the people in battle, or rule over them wisely when at peace.

During the time of Judges, a man called Elimelech lived in the town of Bethlehem with his wife, Naomi, and their two sons. As there was a famine in Israel and little food to eat, Elimelech decided to take his family to live for a while in the land of Moab. There his sons grew up happily, and eventually married Moabite girls. But, while they were in Moab, Elimelech died. So, Naomi was cared for by her two sons and their wives, Orpah and Ruth.

Sadly, not long after the death of Elimelech, both Naomi's sons died, too. So, she was left alone, with her sons' wives, living in a foreign country. Naomi longed to be back in her homeland. So, when she heard that the famine there was over, she decided it was time to move.

Accompanied by Ruth and Orpah, Naomi set out on the road to Israel. As they reached the border of the two countries, Naomi stopped and said to the Moabite girls, "You must go back now, each of you, and return to your own mothers. You are young and you can marry again. May the Lord show kindness to you, as you have shown to me."

The two daughters-in-law wept and clung to Naomi. "We will come with you to your people," they said. But Naomi assured them that they would be better off in Moab. So, Orpah hugged and kissed Naomi, and reluctantly turned round and set off for home.

But Ruth was determined. "Don't tell me to leave you, Naomi," she said. "I will stay with you wherever you go. Your people will be my people, and your God, my God. Only death will separate us now."

Naomi realised that Ruth would not change her mind, so the two women travelled together to Bethlehem. Naomi's friends welcomed her back, and were shocked to hear about the deaths of her husband and sons. They could see that Ruth and Naomi were now very poor. In those days, women could not earn a living and relied on their men to provide for them. The only way they could find food was to go gleaning in the fields. That meant they could follow the reapers, and pick up any stray bits of grain that were left behind.

Luckily, Ruth and Naomi had arrived in Bethlehem at harvest time. "Let me go to the fields and glean barley," Ruth said to Naomi. And off she went.

Ruth and Boaz

Ruth came to the field of a man called Boaz, and there she gleaned barley all day long. Boaz noticed Ruth working hard in his field. "Who is that young woman?" he asked. His workers told Boaz that Ruth was the Moabite girl who had returned with Naomi.

Boaz was a relation of Naomi's husband, Elimelech. He had heard about Ruth and her kindness to Naomi, and he wanted to help her. Boaz told his workers to drop barley on purpose for Ruth to pick up, and he told her always to glean in his field, so that she would come to no harm.

When she returned home, Naomi was surprised at the amount of barley Ruth had gathered. "Where did you find so much?" she asked.

So, Ruth told Naomi about Boaz, and all that he had said to her. "The Lord bless him!" said Naomi. "He is our relative. You will be safe with him."

Ruth gleaned in the fields of Boaz until harvest time was over. Then Naomi told her what to do. "Put on your best clothes and go to the harvest supper. When Boaz has eaten and drunk his fill, go to him. Ask him to care for us and protect us because we are his family."

Although she felt very nervous and shy, Ruth did as Naomi had suggested. Boaz was pleased that the young woman had come to him for help. He wanted to marry Ruth, but knew that there was an even closer relative of Elimelech who lived in the town. That man had the right to buy Elimelech's land and to take care of the two widows. But the other relative told Boaz that he was not interested in dealing with the women, so Boaz was free to do as he liked.

Everyone in town celebrated the marriage of Ruth and Boaz. They were even more delighted when, some time later, Ruth had a baby boy. Now Naomi had a grandson. Little did she realise that this tiny baby was to be the grandfather of a very special man called David.

The Prophet Samuel

In the time when the Judges ruled the Israelites, and Philistines occupied the land, there lived a man called Elkanah. He had two wives called Peninnah and Hannah. Peninnah had both sons and daughters, but Hannah had no children. She longed for a child of her own.

Every year, Elkanah took his wives and children to worship and make sacrifices to God in the temple at Shiloh. Hannah dreaded these happy family outings. She felt miserable and left out without her own children. Also, Peninnah was jealous of Elkanah's love for Hannah, so she was nasty and teased Hannah.

One year when this happened, Hannah was so upset she could not eat. "Don't be sad," said Elkanah, kindly. "I love you. Doesn't that mean more to you than ten sons?"

But Hannah could not be comforted and went to the temple to pray. She knelt down and wept. "O Lord God, please don't forget me," Hannah begged. "I'm so unhappy without a child. If you give me a son, I will give him back to serve you all his life." As she continued to pray, Hannah's lips moved but no sound came out as she was talking privately to God.

The priest of the temple, old Eli, was watching from the doorway. He saw Hannah mouthing words that could not be heard and thought perhaps she had drunk too much wine.

Eli went over to Hannah.

"I'm not drunk, my lord," she said. "I'm very sad, and I've been asking God to help me." Eli felt sorry for Hannah. "Go in peace," he said, "and may God answer your prayer."

After she had prayed, Hannah felt better and was able to eat. When she returned home with Elkanah she felt peaceful and calm.

Some time later, Hannah knew that, at last, she was going to have a child. She was overjoyed when she gave birth to a son. Hannah called the boy Samuel, which means 'asked of God'.

When Samuel was old enough, Hannah kept her promise to God. At the time of the annual sacrifice, she took her little boy to Shiloh.

Hannah reminded Eli of the day she had come to the temple weeping. "I prayed for this child," she said, "and the Lord gave him to me. Now I must give my son back to God to serve here in the temple with you. Please take care of him."

Eli was pleased to have Samuel to keep him company and treated him like a grandson. Eli's own sons made him sad as they were always doing wicked things and did not worship God. So, the priest taught Samuel how to help in the temple, and all about God's law.

Every year, Hannah visited her son and took him a new coat to wear. She missed Samuel dreadfully, but she could not forget her promise to God. Eli prayed that the Lord would give Hannah other children to comfort her, and after a time she had three sons and two daughters.

God calls Samuel

As Samuel grew up, he obeyed Eli in all things. In his old age, Eli could not see well and he was glad to have Samuel close by him. Each night they slept in the temple near the ark of God.

One night, while Samuel was sleeping, he heard a voice calling him, "Samuel! Samuel!"

So, the boy got up and went over to Eli. "Here I am," he said, "you called me."

"I didn't call you," said Eli. "Go back to sleep."

So, Samuel lay down. But then he heard the voice again. Once more Samuel crept over to Eli. "My son," said Eli, "I didn't say a word."

Then, a third time, Samuel heard the voice calling, "Samuel!" This time, when the boy went to Eli, the old priest realised what was happening. He told Samuel that it must be the voice of God calling him.

"If you hear your name again," he told Samuel, "say, 'Speak Lord, your servant is listening.' "

So, Samuel waited. Again he heard his name, so he answered, "I'm here Lord. Your servant is listening." Then God told Samuel that because Eli's sons had been wicked, and Eli had not been strict with them, they would be punished.

The next morning, Eli asked Samuel what God had said to him. Samuel loved the old man and he did not want to hurt him, but Eli insisted. So, Samuel told the priest everything. "He is the Lord," said Eli. "God knows what is best."

After that, God often spoke to Samuel about what was to happen in Israel. Soon, Samuel became known as the prophet of God.

Samuel makes Saul king

All this time, the Philistines continued to be Israel's main enemy, and defeated them in battle many times. As usual, the Israelites started to doubt that God was with them. "Let's bring the ark of God from the temple, and carry it to the battlefield," said the leaders. "Then we will have God's protection from our enemies."

Eli's wicked sons stole the sacred chest from its holy shrine and took it to where the army was camped. When the Philistines realised that Israel's precious ark was amongst them they fought even harder. They slaughtered the Israelites, killed Eli's sons and captured the ark.

The old priest had spent his life protecting the sacred box. When he heard that the precious ark of God was in enemy hands, Eli fell back in shock, broke his neck and died.

Meanwhile, the Philistines took the ark to their temple and placed it next to the statue of their god, Dagon. The next day, they found the statue flat on its face. After that, wherever they put the sacred chest, a terrible illness came over their people. The Philistines grew so terrified of the ark, they decided to send it back to the Israelites. "Let's put the chest on a cart," they said. "Two cows can pull it in whichever direction they choose. If the cows go off towards Israel, we will know that it was their God who brought these illnesses upon us."

So, they tethered the cows to the cart and the animals headed straight back to the Israelites, mooing all the way. There was great rejoicing when the ark came home.

After the death of Eli, Samuel became the
judge to advise and lead the children of Israel.
Samuel gathered the people and spoke to them.
"If you are ever to be rid of the Philistines you
must worship the Lord with all your hearts and
obey his commandments. You can't expect God
to rescue you as long as you serve other gods."
So, the Israelites turned from their wicked ways
and promised to obey God's law. And as long
as Samuel led the people, all through his life
they had victory over the Philistine armies and
kept them from invading Israel's land.

But as Samuel grew old, the Israelites worried
about what would happen when he died. "We
want a king," the people told Samuel. "We need
someone to lead us against our enemies."

Samuel felt hurt by what they said and he
went away to pray. "It's not you they don't
want," God said to Samuel. "It's me. They want
a king to fight for them because they don't trust
me." The Lord told Samuel to give the people a
king, but to warn them what it would mean.

So, the prophet told the Israelites, "If you
have a king he will take your men for his army,
and your women for his palace." Samuel went
on, "He will take your land and your crops for
his own use." But still the people wanted a king
to lead them in battle.

Then God told Samuel to go to a man called
Saul, from the tribe of Benjamin. He would be
the one to conquer the Philistines. No one was
more surprised than Saul when Samuel, the
prophet of God, anointed his head with oil and
announced, "God has chosen you to be the first
king of Israel."

King Saul

Samuel gathered the people together and told them that God had chosen Saul to be king. Saul was a big, tall, strong man and looked very much like a leader. "This is the man that the Lord has chosen," said Samuel. "See, there is no one like him among you." And the Israelites shouted, "Long live the king!"

Then Samuel wrote down all the duties of the new king, and those that would follow him. He told Saul and the people of Israel that if they obeyed God, and kept his commandments, the Lord would help them. But, he warned, if they or their king disobeyed God, and did what they pleased, they would lose God's protection.

Saul was thirty years old when he became king, and he ruled over Israel for forty-two years. At first, some of the Israelites doubted that Saul could lead them, but he soon won their respect by winning a great victory in battle.

Not long after Saul became king, the Ammonites besieged the Israelite city of Jabesh. "Please don't attack us," begged the people of Jabesh. "We will make peace with you." But the fierce Ammonites said they would only agree to a peace treaty if they first blinded every citizen in their right eye! The people of Jabesh were horrified and sent for help all over Israel.

When Saul heard about the Ammonites he was furious. He ordered every tribe of Israel to send him fighting men. Then, having gathered a large army, he went off to the rescue.

At dawn, the Israelite army crept up on the enemy and took them by surprise. They slaughtered the Ammonites, and those that survived were scattered. The people of Jabesh were saved, and Saul became a hero.

Saul was a great soldier king. With his son, Jonathan, he went on to fight many battles against the Philistines who were the worst enemy of all.

Saul disobeys God

During one battle campaign, the Israelites grew very downhearted. They were not properly armed and the Philistine force was huge. Many of Saul's men deserted and went to join the other side. But Jonathan was a brave young warrior. He saw an opportunity to save the day.

At the top of a cliff, a group of Philistine soldiers guarded a narrow pass in the rocks. This led down to the valley where the vast army of the Philistines was camped. "Let's climb up," said Jonathan to his armour-bearer. "Perhaps the Lord will help us capture the pass." The two men secretly climbed up the steep hillside and overpowered the Philistine guards. Then, waving their weapons, the brave, young Israelites appeared at the top of the hill and looked down on the thousands of Philistine soldiers below.

The Philistines looked up. Thinking that Jonathan was leading a huge army against them, they took to their heels and fled.

As time went by, Saul grew very powerful in
Israel. But Samuel still told him what to do.
The prophet was always there to pass on God's
orders, and to remind the king to obey them.
Gradually, however, Saul became very selfish
and wanted his own way.

Saul first disobeyed God's orders when
fighting with the Philistines at Gilgal. Samuel
had told Saul to wait a week before going into
battle, so that the prophet could make a sacrifice
to God before the Israelites fought. But Saul
grew impatient and, without waiting for Samuel,
made the sacrifice himself. So, God was not with
Saul. As a result, the Israelite troops quaked with
fear at the sight of their enemy. Many of them
deserted and only six hundred men were left.

"You have acted foolishly," Samuel told Saul
when he arrived. "If you had obeyed God, he
would have honoured you by allowing your son
to become king when you die. Now, your
kingdom will not last. The Lord will choose a
man who can obey him to take over from you."

Later on, when Saul battled against the
Amelekites he again did not follow the Lord's
commands. Instead he gave in to the wishes of
his people. That day, God spoke to Samuel.
"I'm sorry that I made Saul king," said the
Lord. "He has turned away from me and not
carried out my instructions." When Samuel went
to tackle Saul, the king lied to him. He told the
prophet that he had obeyed God. It became
clear to Samuel that Saul was no longer
the right man to lead Israel.

Samuel anoints David

After a while, God spoke to Samuel again. "Don't worry about Saul any more, but go to see a man called Jesse, the grandson of Ruth and Boaz, in Bethlehem. I have chosen one of his sons to be king."

Samuel was puzzled. "How can I go and choose another king?" he asked God. "Saul will hear about it and kill me."

"Saul does not need to know yet," said the Lord. And he told the prophet what to do. "Take with you an animal to sacrifice, and invite Jesse's family to join you at the feast. You are to anoint the one I tell you."

So, Samuel went to Bethlehem and the people gathered to join him at the sacrifice. When Jesse and his sons arrived, Samuel studied them carefully. He looked at Eliab, the eldest son. He was tall and goodlooking, rather like Saul had been as a young man. "That must be the one God wants as the next king," thought Samuel.

But the Lord said to Samuel, "This is not the right one. You are looking at the outward appearance. I look at a man's heart. I know his thoughts and feelings. That is what is important to me."

So, then Samuel looked at all Jesse's other sons that were present at the feast. But none of them was the one God wanted to anoint as king. "I have seen seven of your sons," said Samuel to Jesse. "Do you have any more?"

Jesse told Samuel that he had one more son, the youngest, who was out looking after the sheep. "Send for him," said Samuel. "We will not begin the feast until he's here, too." So, someone ran to fetch the shepherd boy.

Soon Jesse's young son, David, hurried in to join them all. He was a handsome boy who looked fit and healthy from his life outdoors.

"Anoint him," God told Samuel. "He is the one I have chosen to be the next king." So, the prophet took his horn of olive oil and, in front of everyone, he sprinkled a few drops on to David's head. From that day on, God was with David in a very special way.

The Philistines

David was still very young, and so was not yet ready to be king. But God was preparing him for the time he would eventually take over from Saul. Only David and Samuel knew this. For a while, Saul was to carry on leading the people.

Meanwhile, the Philistines were overrunning Israel yet again, and gathered their armies at a place called Socoh. Saul and the Israelite army camped on a hillside opposite the Philistines and prepared for battle.

Among the Philistines there was a fierce giant of a man, called Goliath. This huge warrior was over nine feet tall and wore a bronze helmet and a coat of heavy chainmail. Waving an enormous spear in his hand, and with a javelin slung on his back, Goliath stood in the valley between the two armies and shouted at the Israelites, "Why do you line up for battle? Choose a man to come down and fight against me. If he kills me, we the Philistines, will become your subjects, but if I kill him, then you will become our subjects and serve us. Send your own champion and we will fight together!"

When Saul and the Israelites saw and heard Goliath, they were afraid, and none of them dare accept his challenge.

Three of David's brothers were in the Israelite army lined up against the Philistines, but David was at home looking after the sheep. One day, Jesse said to David, "Take this corn and these ten loaves to your brothers in the camp. Then come back and tell me how they are."

David took the food and went off to the Israelite army. When he reached the camp, the men were ready for battle. So, David hurried through the lines of soldiers to speak to his brothers. While he was talking with them, Goliath, the Philistine champion, stood forward and shouted out his challenge again.

David asked a nearby soldier, "What reward will be given to the one who kills the Philistine giant, and restores Israel's reputation? Someone must go out and tackle this man that is against the Lord's army."

"The king will give great wealth to the man," the soldiers replied. "He will also give his daughter in marriage and free his whole family from taxation."

David's eldest brother, Eliab, heard him speaking with the other soldiers. "What are you up to?" he asked. "You should be back looking after the sheep, not sneaking up here to watch the battle."

But David again spoke about Goliath to those around him. News of this reached Saul, and he sent for the boy. The king was amazed when David said, "Don't be afraid of this Philistine giant. I will go and fight him."

"But *you* can't tackle this man!" replied Saul. "You are a boy, and he is a trained soldier."

"I have watched over my father's sheep," said David. "Whenever a lion or a bear attacks a sheep from my flock, I kill it. The Lord has saved me from wild animals. Surely, in the same way, he will protect me from this Philistine."

Saul was convinced by what David said. "Go," he said, "and may God be with you."

David fights Goliath

David, dressed only in a tunic, picked five smooth stones from a nearby stream and put them in his shepherd's bag. Then, with his staff in his hand and his sling over his shoulder, David went off to fight Goliath.

The Philistine champion roared with laughter when he saw David approach. "Do you take me for a dog, that you carry only a stick?" he said. "I'll give your flesh to the wild animals."

But David replied, "You come against me with sword, spear and javelin, but I come against you in the name of the Lord Almighty, the God of the armies of Israel. Today, he will give you to me, and I will strike you down and cut off your head." David went on, "Everyone gathered here will know that the battle is in God's hands, and he will give all of you to Israel."

At these words, the angry giant lunged towards the shepherd boy. David quickly reached into his bag and took out a stone. Using his sling, he hurled the little pebble with all his might at Goliath. The stone sank into the giant's forehead and he fell to the ground. David ran forward, took Goliath's sword and cut off his head.

When the Philistines saw that their hero was dead, they turned and ran. But the Israelite army gave chase and slaughtered thousands of them.

Saul sent for David, who stood before the king with Goliath's head in his hands. "Whose son are you, young man?" Saul asked.

"I'm the son of your servant, Jesse, in Bethlehem," answered David.

From then on, Saul was to see a lot more of this brave shepherd boy.

David and Jonathan

Saul was so pleased with David that he invited him to live at court. There, David often played on his harp to soothe Saul when he felt depressed. The king was very moody and, for a time, David's music comforted Saul and made him feel better.

Saul's son, Jonathan, liked David immediately, and it was not long before they had become great friends. David and Jonathan grew so close that they loved each other like brothers.

As David was successful in everything he did, Saul gave him a high rank in the army. This pleased the army officers and the people, as the brave young warrior was very popular. In fact, Saul was beginning to grow a little jealous of David's popularity.

After the death of Goliath, the Israelite women had danced for joy in the streets and had sung, "Saul has slain his thousands, and David his tens of thousands". King Saul had heard this and it had upset him.

Gradually, Saul's jealousy grew worse. Saul was fearful as he could see how everyone loved David, and that God was watching over this fine, handsome man. Overcome by his bad moods, Saul twice hurled a spear at David as he played softly on his harp. Each time, David ducked out of the way, and so escaped death.

As Saul's fear and jealousy grew stronger, so did his desire to kill David. The king sent the young officer on a difficult mission against the Philistines in the hope that he would not survive the battle. But God protected David and, instead, he had a great victory over the enemy.

One of Saul's daughters, Michal, also loved David. The king saw this as a chance to trap his rival. He gave his daughter in marriage to the young hero, hoping that he could later persuade Michal to betray her husband. But, after the wedding, Saul realised that Michal was devoted to David and that angered him even more. So, one day, the king ordered his son, Jonathan, to take soldiers and murder David.

But Jonathan warned his friend, "My father has sent me to kill you. Go into hiding until I can persuade him to calm down."

David did as Jonathan suggested, and the king changed his mind.

So, David lived on to battle further with the Philistines. Again he was successful, and Saul's jealous rages became worse than ever. This time, it was the king's daughter who warned her husband. "If you don't run for your life tonight," Michal told David, "then tomorrow Saul will kill you." And she helped David to escape through the bedroom window.

Then Michal took a statue and put it under the bedclothes. She placed goat's hair at the top to look like David's head. When the soldiers arrived to capture David, Michal said, "My husband is ill, please leave."

The soldiers reported this to Saul, who ordered them to bring in the bed on which David lay. When he saw the statue, and realised his daughter had tricked him, Saul was furious.

"David threatened to kill me if I did not help him," lied Michal. So, Saul believed his daughter and she was not harmed.

David the Outlaw

After he had left Saul's palace, David went to find Samuel at Ramah, and told him all that had happened. But Saul took his soldiers to capture David, and once more he had to flee.

While David was in hiding, Jonathan came to see him. He warned David that Saul was determined to kill him, but promised David that he would always be his friend. "Go in peace," said Jonathan, "for we have sworn friendship with each other." Then the two friends sadly said goodbye. Jonathan returned to court, and David went back to living as an outlaw, away from everyone and everything he knew.

First, David went to a place called Nob, where there were some priests of God. Not realising that David was on the run from Saul, the priests fed him and gave David Goliath's sword to use. When news of this reached Saul, he sent for the priests and had them killed.

David was very distressed when he heard about the priests, so he and his band of supporters went to live in the hills. For a long time, David lived as an outlaw in the wild.

One day, as David was hiding from Saul's men in a cave, Saul himself came into the cave, but did not see David crouched in the darkness. When the king turned his back on him, David crept up to Saul and, with his sword, cut off a corner of Saul's robe. The king did not notice what had happened and left the cave.

Then David went after Saul and called out, "My lord king. Why do you think I am against you?" David held up the piece of robe. "Look!" he said. "Today I could have killed you, but I will not harm my master because he is anointed by God."

When Saul saw David, and heard what he said, he felt sad and ashamed. "You are a better man than I," he replied. "You have treated me well, and I have treated you badly. I know that one day you will be king. Please promise me that you won't harm my family when that time comes." David thought of his friend, Jonathan, and promised Saul. Then the king returned home, and David went back to his cave.

For years, David and his men lived in this way, until they grew weary of it all. During this time, Samuel, the prophet, died and there was great mourning throughout Israel. David grew very downhearted. "The only place I will be safe from Saul," he said, "is among his enemies, the Philistines."

And so that is exactly where David went.

A Philistine leader, called Achish, thought David would make a useful ally against Israel, so he let him live on the borders of his land. In exchange, David and his men went on raids for Achish, and brought back loot from the towns they had plundered. David let Achish think they were raiding Israel, but they were actually looting other people who were also Israel's enemies. There soon came a time, however, when all the Philistines gathered together to fight against Israel.

The Death of Saul

As the Philistines prepared for battle, Achish said to David, "You must accompany me in the army. I want you to be my personal bodyguard." David had no alternative but to agree. The Philistines marched in their thousands to the battleground, and David and his outlaws marched with Achish.

When the other Philistine leaders saw David and his men, they were angry. "What are these Israelites doing here?" they asked Achish. "Send them away, or they will turn against us and fight for the other side." And, although Achish argued to keep David with him, he was forced to send the outlaws back to the border. David was relieved that he did not have to fight against Saul, Jonathan and his own people.

Meanwhile, King Saul had become very nervous. When he saw the size of the Philistine army, he was terrified. Samuel was now dead, so he had no one to turn to. Saul tried asking God for guidance, but he did not get any answers. Saul grew so desperate for Samuel's advice, he decided to go and visit a person who could conjure up the spirits of the dead. He had heard there was a witch at a place called Endor. Saul himself had banned such people in Israel, as they were against God's laws. Therefore, when he went to see the witch, he disguised himself, so she would not recognise him as her king.

"Bring up the spirit of Samuel," Saul
commanded the woman and, after a while, she
did. "What am I to do?" Saul asked Samuel.
"The Philistines are gathered against me and
God has turned away. Please help me."

But Samuel could not help Saul. Sadly, the
spirit answered, "You chose to disobey God
and do as you wanted. Now God has taken
the kingdom from your hands and given it to
David. Tomorrow you will be defeated by
the Philistines and you and your sons will die."

When Saul heard Samuel's words, he collapsed
on the floor in fear. Then, filled with despair,
the king returned to camp. The next day, at a
place called Gilboa, the Philistine army
massacred the Israelites, who fled from their
enemy. Jonathan was killed and the king
himself was badly wounded. Rather than be
murdered by the Philistines, Saul took his own
sword, and killed himself.

A messenger brought the news of defeat to
David and his men. "The Israelites have fled
from battle," said the man. "Many were slain,
and Saul and Jonathan are dead." Then the
messenger gave David the king's crown.

Jonathan was dead! David could not bear to
hear these terrible words. He would never see
his best friend again. David was stunned by the
awful truth. He thought about Saul, too. He
remembered all the good things about the man
who had wanted him dead. After all, Saul had
been his master and king, as well as his enemy.
David was filled with a great sadness, and
grieved for Saul and Jonathan for a long time.

King David

After Saul's death, David became king. He was to become the greatest king that Israel had ever known.

At first, David was only king over a part of Israel, called Judah, which was the tribe to which he belonged. The rest of Israel was ruled by Saul's remaining son, Ishbosheth, who was helped by his army general, Abner.

For a while, there was civil war in Israel, until Abner saw sense and went to join David. Abner also restored Saul's daughter, Michal, to her husband after all their years of living apart. At last, all the tribes of Israel united and asked David to be their king.

Once David had become king over all Israel, he decided to establish a new capital city. The ideal place was the fortified city of Jerusalem, but this did not belong to Israel. The fortress was held by people called the Jebusites, who believed their stronghold was impossible to capture. David, however, had a plan.

There was a tunnel which led from the water supply outside the city right up inside the city walls. "Anyone who conquers the Jebusites will have to use the water shaft to reach them," said David. "We just need to find the way in."

An Israelite soldier, called Joab, was determined to succeed. He found the hidden entrance and, with his men, secretly climbed up the tunnel into the city. There, the men opened the city gates and let in David and the Israelite army. The Jebusites were taken by surprise, and Jerusalem was captured. It became the capital of all Israel, and was known as the City of David.

Once David had settled into his new city, it
was time to make it God's city, too. So, David
brought the sacred ark of God to Jerusalem,
and set it up in the tabernacle. There was great
celebration amongst the Israelites when the ark
came to Jerusalem. David joined the people as
they danced and sang for joy in the streets. He
wrote a poem, or psalm, which he sang to God
in praise:

"Lift up your heads, O you gates;
be lifted up, you ancient doors,
that the King of glory may come in."

David's wife, Michal, who was Saul's
daughter, did not join in the celebration. She
thought her husband, the king, was making a
fool of himself, dancing in the streets. "How
vulgar you looked today, dancing with the slave
girls," she said. "You are too grand to behave
like that."

But David answered his wife, "I was thanking
and praising the Lord, who chose me to be king
rather than your father. My greatness does not
matter. It is God that is important."

David's Kingdom

Once David was king of Israel, the Philistines came in full force to attack him. God told David to lead his army against them, and the Israelites had a great victory. David went on to defeat all his enemies and establish a large kingdom.

When there was peace in the land, David settled down to live in his palace in Jerusalem. One day, he sent for a man called Nathan, who was a prophet of God. "Here I am, living in a beautiful palace," said David, "while the ark of God remains in a tent. Do you think I should build a temple for the ark?"

"Go ahead," said Nathan. "It sounds like a wonderful idea."

But, that night, God spoke to Nathan. He told the prophet that he did not want David to build him a temple. It would be a son of his who built it in the future. "Tell my servant, David, this is what the Lord Almighty says," said God. "I will make you one of the greatest men on earth. I will never take my love away from you as I did from Saul. Your sons, and their sons after them, will be kings of Israel for ever. Your kingdom will never end." Nathan went to David and told him everything that God had said.

When Nathan had gone, David went to the tabernacle and prayed before the ark. He poured out his thanks to the Lord. "How great you are, O Lord! There is no one like you. Thank you for blessing the house of your servant, so that it will continue for ever."

David still missed his friend, Jonathan, and he remembered that he had promised Saul that his family would come to no harm when Saul was dead. "Are there any relatives of Saul or Jonathan still living that I should know about?" he asked his advisers. They sent for an old servant of Saul, called Ziba, who told them that Jonathan's disabled son, Mephibosheth, was still living.

So, David ordered that Mephibosheth be brought before him. The poor, crippled man was terrified and thought David was going to kill him.

But David said, "Don't be afraid. I want to help you. I will give you the land that belonged to your grandfather, Saul. You must come and live at the palace and eat at my royal table."

"Your majesty, I don't deserve your kindness," replied Mephibosheth. "I cannot be of any use to you."

But David looked at the man kindly and said, "You are the son of Jonathan, and he was my dearest friend."

David and Bathsheba

By now, David had everything that he could wish for. He was king of Israel, and lived in a grand palace with his lovely wives and many fine children. But, it seems, this was not enough.

One warm, spring afternoon, David went to keep cool in the room on the roof of his palace. He looked out across the city of Jerusalem. Not far away, in the courtyard of a nearby house, a woman was bathing. David saw that she was very beautiful. "Who is that woman?" David asked a servant. "She is the wife of Uriah, one of your trusty soldiers," answered the servant. "Her name is Bathsheba."

Uriah was away fighting with the army under the command of Joab, David's general. So, David sent for Bathsheba, and made love to her. He did not stop to think that he was disobeying God. By sleeping with another man's wife, he was breaking one of the ten commandments.

Some time later, Bathsheba sent a message to the king, informing him that she was pregnant. As Uriah, her husband, was away fighting for his king, it was clear that this was David's child. Soon everyone would know what the king had done.

David asked Joab, his general, to send Uriah home on leave, so that he could also spend time with his wife. Uriah returned to Jerusalem, and reported the news of battle to his king. But Uriah did not go home. Instead, he spent the night sleeping at the palace gate.

"Why did you not go home to your wife?"
David asked him the next day.

"Your majesty, how could I go and enjoy
myself when the rest of the army is still at war?"
Uriah replied. He was such a loyal soldier, that
no matter what David did to persuade him, he
would not consider himself 'off duty' and go
back to his wife. So, David's plan had failed.

Then David did something even worse. He
sent Uriah back to war, and ordered Joab to
place him in the front line of battle, where the
fighting was at its most fierce. As a result,
Uriah was killed. When David heard that Uriah
was dead, he was glad. Now he could marry
Bathsheba.

But God was angry with David. He sent
Nathan the prophet to speak to the king.

Nathan told David a story. "There were two
men living in the same town," he said. "One
was rich and the other was poor. The rich man
had many flocks, but the poor one had just one
little lamb which was very precious to him."
Nathan went on. "The rich man had a visitor,
and he wanted to feed him with roast meat.
But, instead of killing one of his own flock, he
killed the poor man's only lamb."

"That's terrible!" said David. "The rich man
deserves to die."

"You are that man!" cried Nathan. "God took
you as a poor shepherd boy and gave you
everything. Yet you took Uriah's precious wife.
You have disobeyed God, and now sadness and
trouble will come to your family, too. Although
God has forgiven your sin, the child that is
born to you and Bathsheba will die!" said
Nathan. Then 'he left the palace.

David and Absalom

After Nathan had left, David felt sad and ashamed. He knew he had done wrong. When Bathsheba had a baby boy that was weak and sickly, David prayed for the child to live. But, although God forgave David his wrongdoing, as Nathan had prophesied, Bathsheba's baby died. David was sorry for the suffering he had caused, and learned not to disobey God.

Some time later, Bathsheba became pregnant again. This time, she had a son who was strong and healthy, and his parents called him Solomon. "God loves this child," Nathan told David. "He will always be with him." So, the birth of Solomon brought David great joy. But, another son was to bring the king great sorrow.

As well as Bathsheba, David had several wives, and by them the king had many children. But there was often quarrelling and rivalry between the families. The eldest of David's sons, Amnon, behaved in a cruel way to his half-sister, Tamar. Although David was angry, he did not punish Amnon as he should have done. So, Tamar's real brother, Absalom, took matters into his own hands, and swore to get revenge for the way his sister had been treated.

Two years later, Absalom organised a large party out in the countryside, and invited all the royal princes to attend. At the feast, he ordered his servants to get Amnon drunk, and then kill him. This they did. After the murder, Absalom fled from Israel and went into hiding.

The king was horrified at what had happened, and he cried bitterly for both his sons. He missed Absalom, although he could not forgive the terrible thing he had done.

After two years had gone by, David allowed Absalom to come back and live in Jerusalem. But he still refused to see him and forgive him for the death of his half-brother. Absalom was upset by his father's attitude. Now that Amnon was dead, he was the next in line to be king. Absalom began to make himself as popular as he could with the people, and soon this handsome young man had won a lot of support.

Four years later, many of the people of Israel began to think that Absalom would make a very good king. However, Absalom was not going to wait for David to die before he inherited the kingdom. He planned to take it from his father as soon as he could.

Absalom went to Hebron, and raised an army to fight for him. The king's son sent messengers to the leaders of the tribes of Israel, saying, "When you hear the trumpets sound, shout 'Absalom is king!' "

Soon, the king's son had a great following, and even David's most trusted friend and adviser, Ahithophel, had gone to join the other side.

The Death of Absalom

A messenger came and told David, "The people of Israel are going over to Absalom. He intends to make himself king."

When David heard the news, he decided the best thing to do was to flee from Jerusalem. "We must leave immediately," he said, "or Absalom will overpower us, and there will be terrible bloodshed in the city."

So, all the king's household and his loyal soldiers marched out of Jerusalem towards the desert. The priests carried with them the ark of God. But the king turned to two of the priests, Zadok and Abiathar. "Take the ark back to Jerusalem where it belongs," he said. "It may be that the Lord will restore my kingdom to me. Also take your sons back with you. They can act as my spies and tell me Absalom's plans."

So, the priests carried the precious ark back into the city, and David very sadly carried on his journey. As he travelled, he met Hushai, another of his close advisers. "You can help me if you return to Jerusalem," David told his friend. "Pretend you are on Absalom's side, and report everything that is said to Zadok and Abiathar. Their sons are my spies, and they will bring me news."

So, Hushai went to the city and joined Absalom. There he gave false advice to Absalom, and so delayed any immediate attack on David's household. Absalom decided to wait and gather a larger army to fight his father.

Meanwhile, David's spies told him what Absalom was planning, and his supporters in the nearby farmlands had brought out food and drink to refresh the king and his soldiers. After they had eaten and slept well, David and his men felt much stronger and ready to fight. But everyone begged David to remain behind. "You are too precious to risk in battle," said his commanders.

Reluctantly, David agreed. As Joab, his general, led the army away, David said, "Be gentle with Absalom, for my sake."

So, near the River Jordan, the two armies lined up for battle, and the fighting began. That day, David's men defeated the army of Israel that had gathered against them, and Absalom's men started to flee. As the king's son was riding away through the forest, his long hair caught in the branches of a tree. The mule bolted, and Absalom was left dangling, unable to move.

A soldier rushed to tell Joab where Absalom was. "Why didn't you kill him?" cried Joab.

"I could not harm the king's son," replied the soldier. "It would be more than my life was worth."

But, despite what David had said, Joab found where Absalom was hanging, and speared him to death. Then the general sounded the trumpet and summoned his army. The rebellion was over, and David's kingdom was saved.

When he heard that his son was dead, David cried out, "O my son, Absalom! My son, my son... if only I had died instead of you!"

And so, although it was a day of victory for the army, it was also a day of terrible mourning, too.

David chooses Solomon

After a while, David realised that he must stop mourning, and show his loyal supporters that he was grateful for the victory they had given him. Also, the Israelites who had gone over to Absalom invited David back to be king. So, David returned in triumph to Jerusalem to rule over Israel once again.

As David grew older, he became ill and was incapable of fighting, and even ruling the country properly. So, there came a time when one of his remaining sons had to become king in his place. Now that Absalom was dead, David's eldest son was Adonijah. He was supported by the army general, Joab, and Abiathar, one of David's chief priests. But Nathan the prophet and Zadok, another priest, knew that Solomon was the one whom God wanted to be king.

Nathan went to see Bathsheba, Solomon's mother. "Have you heard that Adonijah has proclaimed himself king, without David knowing it?" he asked her. "You must save your own life and that of your son, Solomon, by taking my advice." Then Nathan told Bathsheba to speak to David, and remind him of the promise he had made that Solomon would be king.

So, Bathsheba went to David. "My lord, you yourself swore to me by the Lord your God that Solomon would become king after you. But now Adjonijah is planning to make himself king. All of Israel is waiting for you to decide who will rule after you."

While Bathsheba was still speaking, Nathan the prophet came to see David and told him the same thing. When he heard it from both of them, David said to Bathsheba, "I will carry out what I promised to you, by the Lord God of Israel. Solomon, your son, will be king after me, and he will sit on my throne in my place."

So, David ordered that Solomon should be set on David's own mule and led through the city. Then, Zadok the priest and Nathan the prophet were to anoint Solomon king over Israel. David went on, "Blow the trumpet and shout, 'Long live King Solomon!'. I have appointed him ruler over Israel and Judah."

Zadok and Nathan quickly did as the king had ordered, and the people danced and sang in the streets. It was too late for Adonijah. Solomon was king at David's command.

During his life, David wrote many poems, or songs, to tell God how he was feeling. Some are happy and full of thanks and praise. Others show that, like all of us, he was sometimes angry, sad or depressed. These poems are called 'psalms' and are collected together, with others, in the book of Psalms in the Bible.

King Solomon

When David handed over his kingdom to
Solomon, he gave him advice about how
to be a good king. Above all, he reminded
Solomon that he and all his descendants should
obey God. Then, after ruling Israel for forty
years, David died.

At the beginning of his reign, God appeared
to Solomon in a dream and asked the king what
he desired most. Solomon replied, "O Lord my
God, give your servant a wise heart to govern
your people and to sort out right from wrong."

God was pleased that Solomon had not asked
for riches, or other selfish things. "I will do what
you have asked," said the Lord. "I will make
you wiser than anyone else that has ever lived
before or after you. I will also give you what
you have not asked for. You will be the richest
and most respected king ever known and, if you
obey me, I will give you a long life."

Solomon woke up and realised he had been
dreaming, but he knew that the Lord was with
him. So, he went to worship at the sacred ark of
God, and then gave a huge feast for his court.

God did give Solomon great wisdom, and he
wrote down many of his wise sayings and wrote
a thousand songs. His subjects came to him for
justice, and he listened carefully and was always
very fair.

One day, two women were brought before Solomon. They were arguing loudly and were very upset. "Your majesty," said one of them, "this woman and I live in the same house. Not long ago we both had babies. One night, she accidentally lay on her baby, and it suffocated and died. So, while I was sleeping, she got up, took my baby from my side, and put her own dead baby next to me." The woman went on, "When I woke up I thought my baby had died. But when I looked at the child's face, I saw it was not my own child, but hers!"

"No!" cried the other woman. "The living baby is my son. Your child is dead!" Then the two women again started to argue and shout.

"So," said Solomon, "you are both claiming that this baby is your own." Then he thought for a moment. "Bring me a sword!" he called out to his servant. Then he commanded, "Cut this baby in two, so each woman can have half."

The first woman gasped in horror at the thought of the baby being killed. "Please, your majesty," she said, "don't kill the baby. Give the child to her, but let him live!"

However, the second woman said, "Yes, cut it in half. Neither of us shall have him."

Then the king made his judgement. "Don't kill the baby," he ordered his servant. "I wanted to find out who the real mother was. The child belongs to the first woman. She would rather give her baby away than have it harmed."

Everyone who was present at the time marvelled at how clever Solomon had been at discovering the truth. News of this judgement spread throughout Israel, and everyone was amazed at the great wisdom of their king.

Solomon builds the Temple

With his great wisdom and knowledge, King Solomon was able to make clever business deals as well as wise decisions about government. So, the king grew very rich.

Thanks to his father, David, the kingdom of Israel had peace from its enemies. So, Solomon did not have to worry about wars, and could spend time on improving his country instead. He decided to build a splendid palace for his court. In it there was a grand throne room, with an ivory throne covered in gold, and a great banqueting hall, where the guests ate from plates of pure gold and drank from golden cups. The king's court was huge, and ate enormous amounts of food. The people of Israel had to take turns in providing all the cattle and crops that Solomon needed for his palace life.

But the most important thing that Solomon wanted to do with his enormous wealth was to build a beautiful temple in which to put the sacred ark of God. It was to be the most magnificent building that anyone had ever seen. Solomon began by writing to the King of Tyre to order the best cedar wood that his country could provide. "The Lord has given me rest from my enemies," wrote Solomon. "I intend, therefore, to build a temple for God. So, give orders for the cedars of Lebanon be cut for me."

And Hiram, King of Tyre, organised for thousands of cedar and pine logs to be floated in rafts down the sea to Israel.

As well as the finest wood, Solomon ordered the most expensive materials from all over his kingdom to be used for God's house. Eighty thousand craftsmen worked at the best quality stone, cutting and shaping it underground so that the noise of their hammers would not disturb the peace and quiet of the temple site.

Inside the temple, a special inner sanctuary was created for the ark. The walls were covered with pure gold, and skilled workers created ornaments of burnished bronze.

The building of the temple took many years to complete. When it was finally finished, Solomon held a great ceremony to bring the ark to the house of God. Watched by all the leaders of Israel, the priests and Levites carried the sacred ark into the inner sanctuary. As the priests left the holy place, a great cloud filled the temple and everyone felt God's presence around them.

Solomon prayed, "Praise be to the Lord, who has never failed us. May we always worship God and obey him."

The king praised God for a long time as he dedicated the temple to the Lord. Then Solomon and the Israelite leaders offered thousands of sacrifices to God on the altar.

God was pleased with Solomon. Again he appeared to the king in a dream. He told Solomon that as long as he and his family worshipped him and no other gods, they would be blessed and rule over Israel for ever.

The Queen of Sheba

As God had promised, King Solomon became the richest and most respected king that ever lived. Kings and leaders from all over the world requested an audience with him so that they could listen to his great wisdom, and see his immense wealth. These visitors brought with them presents from their own lands.

Solomon also traded with other countries. With King Hiram of Tyre, he built a navy of merchant ships which went on long voyages to other lands bringing back gold, silver, copper, ivory and precious jewels.

The Queen of Sheba heard about this famous, rich and wise king of Israel. She, too, was wealthy and clever. The queen decided that she would pay a visit to King Solomon, and put his wisdom to the test.

So, the Queen of Sheba travelled hundreds of miles from her country to Jerusalem. She brought with her a great caravan of camels, carrying rare spices, precious jewels and large quantities of gold. The queen had some difficult questions she wanted to ask Solomon, and hoped that this wise king would be able to answer them.

When the queen saw the splendour of Solomon's palace and courtiers, it was beyond all she had ever imagined. After she had spoken about many things with Solomon and watched him worship the Lord in the temple, she was overwhelmed by it all.

"Everything I heard about your wisdom and achievements is true!" the queen said to Solomon. "But I did not believe it until I saw and heard for myself. How happy your people must be to listen to such wisdom every day! Praise be to the Lord, your God, who has placed you on the throne of Israel."

Then the Queen of Sheba gave Solomon all the fabulous presents she had brought with her. Never before or since had the king seen so many rare spices. Solomon, in turn, gave the queen beautiful gifts to take back with her. Then, amazed by all she had experienced, the Queen of Sheba and her retinue made the long journey back home.

Solomon's Wives

Despite all the wealth that Solomon possessed, there came a time when the king was spending more than he earned. Life at the palace was very expensive, and Solomon needed enormous amounts of money to maintain all the beautiful buildings in the city. Whenever he was short of money, Solomon asked his subjects to pay higher taxes and, as the people became very poor, this gradually made the king unpopular.

Also, Solomon had many wives. They came from all the different countries in and around the kingdom. These wives were costly to keep and, worst of all, they worshipped foreign gods. As he grew older, Solomon became influenced by his different wives, and built them places of worship for their gods. He began to turn away from the true God that he had always obeyed.

The Lord was angry and sad when he saw that Solomon was disobeying him, and also treating his people harshly in order to satisfy his greed. After all, he had given the king everything he could ever want.

"Solomon," said God, "I promised to give the kingdom of Israel to all your descendants as long as you obeyed and worshipped me. But you have turned away, and do not keep my commandments. Now I will tear the kingdom from your son. But for the sake of your father, David, I will leave a small part for your family."

The Kingdom is divided

At this time, there was a young man called Jeroboam working in Jerusalem. With other workmen, he was repairing the walls of the city. Solomon noticed how hard Jeroboam worked and was impressed. So, he told his foreman to put Jeroboam in charge.

Jeroboam was pleased to be promoted as he was an ambitious man. One day, as he was walking home he met Ahijah, a prophet of God. Ahijah was wearing a new cloak. As he approached Jeroboam, the prophet suddenly took off his new cloak and tore it into twelve pieces. "Jeroboam," he said, "take ten pieces of this cloak for yourself." The young man was amazed. "God is going to tear the kingdom of Israel from Solomon, and give ten tribes to you. But for the sake of his servant, David, two tribes of Israel will be left for Solomon's son to inherit." Then Ahijah told Jeroboam, "God is going to make you king over these ten tribes, and give them to your descendants as long as you obey his commands and worship him always." Then, the prophet went on his way.

At first, Jeroboam could not believe what he had heard. But the more he thought about it, the more Jeroboam liked the idea. In fact, he decided not to wait until Solomon was dead. Jeroboam began to plot to seize Solomon's kingdom immediately.

Solomon, however, heard about these schemes, and Jeroboam had to flee to Egypt for safety.

After ruling over Israel for forty years, Solomon died. Then his son, Rehoboam, became king. Rehoboam was young and indecisive, and he asked all those around him for advice about how to rule. In the end, he took bad advice and acted cruelly towards the people of the northern tribes. This made them rebel against him, and they wanted Jeroboam to be their king instead.

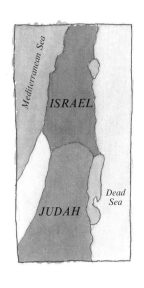

The only two tribes of Israel still loyal to Rehoboam were the tribes of Judah and Benjamin, in the south. Now the country was split in two. The north was called Israel and the south was called Judah.

King Jeroboam set up his headquarters at Shechem, in the north. But, he was worried that his people would still want to travel south to worship at the temple in Jerusalem. If they did this, they might change sides and go over to Rehoboam. So, in order to keep his tribes happy, Jeroboam set up shrines in Bethel and Dan. Golden calves were made and placed on the shrines as gods to be worshipped. Jeroboam even appointed priests who were not from the tribe of Levites (the tribe chosen by God to be priests). As a result, the Israelites of the north turned away from the Lord.

Then Jeroboam's son became ill. So, the king sent his wife to visit the prophet, Ahijah, to ask God if his son would get well. But God was very angry with the way Jeroboam had disobeyed him. Ahijah said to the woman, "Tell your husband that God says, 'I tore the kingdom from Solomon and gave it to you. But you have not obeyed me. You have set up false gods and worshipped them. Because of this, I am going to bring disaster upon your family.' "

King Ahab and Queen Jezebel

It all happened as God had said. Jeroboam's sick son died but, years later, another son, Nadab, became king. He was murdered by a rival who killed every member of Jeroboam's family. No one survived. After this, many kings came and went in both Israel and Judah, but none of them were great men of God.

Then an army general, called Omri, became king of Israel. He was a good soldier, but he was not guided by God. Omri built a new capital for Israel at Samaria, but still continued to worship false gods. When Omri died, his son, Ahab, became king.

King Ahab was more wicked than any other king before him. Not only did he worship false gods, but he married an evil princess, called Jezebel, who worshipped the god Baal. Once she was queen, Jezebel influenced her husband, and he began to worship Baal, too. He built a temple to Baal in Samaria, and allowed hundreds of prophets of Baal to live in the land of Israel. As a result, the people turned away from God even more.

Jezebel was determined to wipe out any worship of the God of Israel, and she ordered that the prophets of God be put to death. Many of them had to flee for their lives, and hide away secretly in caves.

There was at this time a prophet of God called Elijah. The Lord was so angry with Ahab, he sent Elijah to speak to the king.

Bravely, Elijah told Ahab, "For the next few years, the Lord will bring a drought on this land. No rain will fall again until I tell you. You will learn who is the true God of Israel."

So there was no rain. Soon the crops began to wither and die, and there was a shortage of food throughout the land. Ahab and Jezebel were furious with Elijah, and wanted to kill him.

After he had warned Ahab, God told Elijah to leave the city and hide from the king at the Cerith brook, east of the River Jordan. Each day, God sent large black ravens to Elijah, clutching meat and bread in their claws. So, Elijah was able to eat this food and drink the water from the brook.

When the brook dried up, God spoke to Elijah. "Go at once to Zarephath, in Sidon," he said. "A widow lives there and she will feed you." Elijah left Israel, and went to find the widow.

Outside the town of Zarephath, a poor woman was collecting sticks for her fire. Elijah knew that she was the widow, and asked her for something to eat and drink. But, although she was happy to fetch some water, the widow told Elijah she had very little to eat herself. "I have only a handful of flour in a jar and a little oil in a jug. It's only enough for one more meal for my son and me. Then we will die."

Elijah told the woman to use that to make bread for the three of them. "Don't worry," he said. "The Lord says that the jar of flour and the jug of oil will not run dry until the day he sends rain on the land." And God's promise came true. Elijah lived with the widow and her son, and there was always enough to feed them.

Elijah and the Prophets of Baal

After three years of terrible drought, God told Elijah to speak to Ahab once again to tell him that, at last, he would send rain to Israel.

When they met, Ahab accused Elijah of causing Israel's troubles. However, Elijah told Ahab, "You and your fathers have not obeyed the Lord's commands, and have worshipped Baal. Summon the people of Israel to meet me on Mount Carmel, and bring with you Jezebel's four hundred and fifty prophets of Baal."

On the mountainside, Elijah called out to the people and the prophets of Baal, "How long will you waver between two opinions? When are you going to make up your minds about who you worship? Either follow Baal, or follow God."

Then he told the people to bring two bulls and place each on some wood. They were to make one bull a sacrifice to Baal, and Elijah would use the other as a sacrifice to God. "You will call on the name of Baal, and I will call on the name of the Lord," he said. "The god who sets fire to the wood is the true God."

Everyone thought this was a good idea. So, they set up the altars with the wood ready to light. Then the prophets of Baal called upon their god to send fire to burn up their sacrifice. But nothing happened. "O Baal, answer us!" they cried as they danced around the altar.

At noon, Elijah began to taunt them. "Shout louder, perhaps he can't hear you. Maybe he's gone out, or he's fast asleep somewhere!" And the prophets of Baal shouted louder, and frantically slashed themselves with spears and swords. But by evening, still there was nothing.

Then Elijah said to the people, "Come over here to me." So, they gathered round Elijah.

Using twelve stones, each one to represent a tribe of Israel, Elijah made an altar. Then he dug a trench round the altar, and placed the wood in the middle with the bull on the top ready to be sacrificed. "Fill four large jars with water and pour it on the offering and the wood," said Elijah. So, the people did as he said. Elijah told them to do this three times until the water ran down the altar and filled the trench.

When the sacrifice was soaked with water, Elijah stepped forward and called out, "O Lord God of Abraham, Isaac and Israel, prove today that you are God in Israel."

Suddenly, as the crowds watched, flames lit up the altar. The fire was so fierce that it burned up the wood, sacrifice, stones and soil. The intense heat even dried up the water in the trench. The people were amazed. They fell on their faces, shouting, "The Lord – he is God! He is the true God!" Then Elijah ordered the Israelites to seize the prophets of Baal, and put them to death. He wanted nothing to remain in the land that would turn the people from the Lord.

Elijah on Mount Sinai

After the contest on Mount Carmel, Elijah said to Ahab, "Go home and eat. Soon it will rain." So, Ahab began his journey back home. But Elijah and his servant climbed to the top of the mountain. There, Elijah prayed. After a while he said to his servant, "Go and look towards the sea."

"There is nothing there," his servant replied. Six more times the servant did as Elijah had said, and each time there was nothing. The seventh time Elijah's servant said, "There is a small cloud rising from the sea. It's about the size of a man's hand."

So Elijah said, "Go and tell Ahab to hurry home in his chariot if he wants to get there before the rain starts." Meanwhile, the sky grew black with clouds and the wind began to blow. The rain was on its way. Ahab rode full speed in his chariot towards his palace at Jezreel. Elijah suddenly felt so joyful and full of God's strength that he hitched up his long robes, tucked them into his belt, and ran ahead of Ahab all the way back to the city.

When Jezebel heard what had happened to her prophets at Mount Carmel, she was out of her mind with rage. She sent a message to Elijah. "Tomorrow, just as you killed my prophets, I promise I will kill you!"

Elijah, who was normally very brave, suddenly felt afraid. He ran for his life from the city, and fled into the desert. There, tired and hungry, he fell exhausted under a broom tree.

Elijah was so worn out from struggling on alone, he cried out, "I've had enough, Lord. I might as well be dead!" Then he fell asleep.

Suddenly, Elijah felt someone touch his arm. Then he heard a voice saying, "Get up and eat." When Elijah opened his eyes, he saw a loaf of bread and a jar of water on the ground. So he ate and drank, and felt refreshed. Strengthened by the food, Elijah journeyed on. At last, he reached Mount Sinai, the mountain where God had spoken to Moses and given his laws to the children of Israel all those years before.

"What are you doing here, Elijah?" asked God. Elijah told God everything that had happened, and how alone he felt. "I am the only prophet left," he said, "and Jezebel wants to kill me." Then Elijah waited for God to speak to him and guide him.

As Elijah stood on the mountainside, a great wind blew up and howled around him. But the Lord did not speak to him in the wind. Soon, the mountain began to shake and tremble, but God did not speak to his prophet through the earthquake. After that there was a fire. But God did not speak through the fire. Then, after the fire, Elijah heard a gentle whisper. He knew that this was the voice of God. Elijah was filled with awe and wonder, and pulled his cloak over his face. "You are not alone, Elijah," said God. "There are another seven thousand people in Israel who have not worshipped Baal and are loyal to me. Your work is not over yet. But I will give you a helper. Go and anoint Elisha. He will be prophet after you."

Naboth's Vineyard

Some time later, King Ahab was wandering in his palace garden in Jezreel when he had an idea. "How lovely it would be to have a vegetable garden here!" he thought. "I just need a little more land." Next door to the palace was a vineyard. It belonged to a good man called Naboth.

So, Ahab went to visit Naboth. "Let me have your vineyard to use as a vegetable garden," he said to him. "In exchange, I will give you another vineyard or, if you prefer, I will pay you what it's worth."

But Naboth did not want to sell or exchange his vineyard. It had always been in his family. "Your majesty, God gave this land to my ancestors. However much you offer me, I cannot sell it. I must pass it on to my sons," he said.

Ahab went away feeling very angry and disappointed. When he returned to the palace, he lay on his bed sulking and would not eat his supper. "What's the matter?" asked Jezebel. "Why are you so gloomy?"

Ahab told the queen about Naboth and the vineyard. "I don't believe it!" cried Jezebel. "You are the king of Israel. I will make sure you have what you want. Now come and eat."

Jezebel hatched up a plot to get rid of Naboth. If he would not hand over his land, then he would have to go. Jezebel wrote letters to all the important people in the city. She signed them with Ahab's name, and sealed them with his royal seal.

In the letters, she ordered the officials to organise a public holiday and gather all the people to a meeting. "Put Naboth in a prominent place," she wrote, "and seat two scoundrels opposite him, and have them accuse Naboth of cursing both God and the king. Then let the people take Naboth and stone him to death for these crimes."

The leaders who received the letters were frightened of the king, so they did as they were ordered. Poor, innocent Naboth and his sons were killed. "Now," thought Jezebel, "Ahab can have his wish." When Ahab heard that Naboth was dead, he took over the vineyard.

But God saw what had happened, and he was angry. He sent Elijah to speak to Ahab. The prophet found the king in the vineyard. "So, you have found me, my enemy!" said Ahab.

"Yes," said Elijah. "I have found you because yet again you have been wicked and disobeyed God. You have murdered a man and seized his property, and the Lord has seen it all. Because of your evil ways, God is going to bring disaster on you and your family, as he did to Jeroboam. You and your vile wife, Jezebel, will have a sudden death and, after you have gone, your sons will not reign over Israel."

When Ahab heard these words, he was afraid and ashamed. He went without food, and was sad and depressed. The king knew that he had sinned, and he was very sorry.

God saw that Ahab was truly ashamed of himself, so he decided that he would not punish the king immediately.

Elijah and the Chariot of Fire

After Elijah had anointed Elisha, the younger man travelled with Elijah everywhere, helping him and learning all that he could. Elijah was now an old man, and soon it would be time for Elisha to become God's prophet instead.

One day, as they walked along together, they both sensed that the time was drawing near when they would have to part, and God would take Elijah to be with him.

On the road from Gilgal, Elijah told Elisha that the Lord had told him to go to Bethel. He suggested that Elisha stayed where he was, but Elisha said he would not leave his master. So, the two men went to Bethel together. There they met some other prophets of God, who asked Elisha if he knew that the Lord would take Elijah away that day. Elisha refused to talk about it.

Elisha then accompanied Elijah to Jericho where the same thing happened. After this, Elijah asked Elisha to remain in Jericho while he travelled on to the River Jordan, but Elisha would not be parted from the old man.

When they reached the edge of the River Jordan, the two men stopped. Elijah took his cloak, rolled it up and used it like a staff to strike the water. And, just as with Joshua and Moses before him, the water parted and the two men were able to cross to the other side. Not far away, the prophets of Jericho had watched all that had happened.

When they reached the opposite side of the river, Elijah turned to Elisha and asked, "What can I do for you before I am taken from you?"

Elisha replied, "I would like to inherit your spirit. In fact, to be as strong for God as you are I would need a double portion of your spirit."

"You have asked a difficult thing," said Elijah. "But if you actually see me taken from you, it will be yours."

Suddenly, there was a glow in the sky. What seemed like a fiery chariot drawn by horses of fire appeared between them. Then Elisha saw Elijah swept up and away from him in a great whirlwind. As Elisha watched in amazement, he cried out, "My father! My father! Don't leave me!" But, gradually, Elijah and the chariot disappeared from view, and Elisha was all alone.

Elisha felt very sad. He had lost his friend and master. Then he saw Elijah's cloak lying on the floor. He picked it up and, carrying the precious garment with him, he walked back to the river. "Is God with me now?" he wondered. Just as Elijah had done, Elisha rolled the cloak up and struck the water with it. And, as before, the waters of the river parted, and Elisha was able to cross to the other side.

When the Jericho prophets saw this, they said, "As he was with Elijah, God is now with Elisha."

The Prophet Elisha

After Elijah had died, Elisha became the main prophet in Israel. He travelled around preaching to the people about God. Everyone liked Elisha. He was kind and helpful, and listened to their problems.

One day, a poor widow came to Elisha in a terrible state. Her husband had died, leaving her with his debts. The man to whom she owed money insisted that if she did not pay the debt, he would take her two young sons to work as slaves.

"I want to help you," said Elisha. "Tell me, what do you have left in your house that you can sell?"

"There's nothing left except a little oil," said the woman sadly.

Elisha prayed to God for help. Then he said, "Ask all your neighbours to give you any spare jars or containers that they have. Try to borrow as many as possible."

So, the widow did as the prophet had said. Then Elisha told the woman to go inside her house with her sons and shut the door. "Take the oil that you have, and pour it into the spare jars," he said. "As each one gets full, move on to the next container until every single one of them is filled." The widow poured the tiny amount of oil into a jar, and it just kept flowing. The oil flowed until all the jars were full. When the last container had been filled, the oil ran out.

The woman ran to tell Elisha what had happened. "Now, go and sell the oil," he said. "Then you can pay your debts, and you and your sons can live on the money that is left."

Some time later, Elisha went to Shunem to speak about God. A rich woman who lived there invited him to her home for a meal. After that, each time Elisha visited Shunem he was a guest at the same house.

The rich woman said to her husband, "Let's build an extra room on our house for Elisha, so that whenever he travels this way he has somewhere to stay." The husband agreed, so Elisha had his own room with a bed, a chair, a table and a lamp.

The prophet was very grateful to the rich woman, and wanted to thank her in some way.

"All the woman really wants is a son," said his servant. "She would like a baby boy."

Elisha knew that God wanted to help him repay the rich woman. "This time next year," he said to her, "you will hold a son in your arms."

The woman was astonished at what the prophet said. But, the following year, she did have a baby boy. The baby grew up into a strong, healthy child. But, one day, as he was out in the fields helping his father with the reaping, the boy felt ill.

"My head! My head hurts!" he told his father. A servant rushed home with the boy, and his mother nursed him. But, at noon, the child died. The woman did not tell her husband. She placed her son on the bed in Elisha's room, and set off to find the prophet.

Elisha quickly went to the boy, and prayed to God to help him. Then he climbed on to the bed and gently stretched himself out over the child. After a while, the boy sneezed seven times and opened his eyes. "Here is your son," Elisha told the Shunammite woman. "He is alive again."

Elisha and Naaman the Leper

For some time after Elijah had died, King Ahab continued to be king of Israel. The king of Judah at this time was a man called Jehoshaphat. He persuaded Ahab to join with him in a battle against the Syrians. Although Ahab was warned against it, he chose to fight alongside Jehoshaphat. As a result, Ahab was killed, and his army was scattered.

The Syrians were a constant enemy to Israel, and often made raids on the country, carrying off the Israelite people and their possessions. The powerful commander of the Syrian army, Naaman, had captured an Israelite girl, and had given her to his wife as a slave.

Although he was a brave and well-respected soldier, Naaman had a problem. He had a disease called leprosy, for which there was no cure. One day, the Israelite girl said to her mistress, "If only my master would see the prophet Elisha, in Israel. He would cure him of his leprosy."

When his wife told Naaman what the girl had said, the commander asked his king if he could visit Israel to find the prophet. "By all means go," said the Syrian king. "I will write a letter to the king of Israel." So, Naaman set off for Samaria, taking with him much silver and gold.

The king of Israel opened the letter from the king of Syria. It read, "I am sending my servant, Naaman, to you, so that you can cure him of his leprosy."

The Israelite king was terrified. "Does he think that I am God!" he exclaimed. "How can I cure this man of leprosy? He is obviously looking for a reason to pick a quarrel with me!"

But news of all this reached Elisha, and he sent a message to the king of Israel. "Send the Syrian to me," he said, "and he will know that there is a prophet of God in Israel."

So, with all his horses and chariots, Naaman, the Syrian commander, arrived at the door of Elisha's house. But the prophet did not come out to greet him. He sent his servant with a message, saying, "Go and wash yourself seven times in the River Jordan, and you will be healed."

Naaman was furious. "Well!" he said. "I thought that at least he would come out to greet me and call upon the name of his God, wave his hands over me and cure my disease. The rivers of Syria are better than this filthy River Jordan!" And he went away.

But Naaman's servant was wise. "If Elisha had asked you to do something really hard," he said, "you would have made an effort to do it. Why not do this simple thing; it can't harm you."

Naaman thought about it, and knew that his servant was right. So, he went to the River Jordan, and did exactly as Elisha had ordered. After he had dipped himself in the river for the seventh time, Naaman's skin was healed and all signs of the leprosy had disappeared.

So, Naaman returned to Elisha to thank him. "Now I know that the God of Israel is the true God," said Naaman. "Please accept these gifts of gold and silver."

But Elisha would not take the gifts. "I am God's servant," he said. "He has cured you."

The Prophets Amos and Hosea

After King Ahab of Israel had died, his son, Joram, became king with Jezebel as Queen mother. Joram was no better than his father, so a man called Jehu made himself king instead. Then, just as Elijah had prophesied, all of Ahab's family were killed.

Years later, Jehu's great grandson, King Jeroboam II, made Israel strong again. But, although Jeroboam was a powerful king, he did not obey God.

So, God sent a prophet, called Amos, to Israel to remind the people about God's laws. Amos was a shepherd from the southern kingdom of Judah, and he travelled to Israel to sell his wool. Amos looked around the marketplace at Bethel and saw that the traders were dishonest and cheated their customers. So, he spoke out against them and warned them that punishment would come upon Israel if they did not mend their ways.

"You cheat by using false weights, and you make your prices too high for the poor and needy," he cried. "If people can't pay their debts, you take their clothes from them, or make them your slaves." Amos went on, "This is not how God told you to behave. God chose Israel from all the nations of the earth. He brought you out of slavery in Egypt, and has protected you from your enemies. But you have not obeyed the Lord, and he will punish you for your sins."

But the people did not want to listen or change their ways. So, Amos left Israel and returned south to his home in Judah.

As the people of Israel had ignored Amos, God asked a prophet from their homeland to warn them to change their ways. His name was Hosea.

Hosea was married to a pretty girl, called Gomer, whom he loved very much. Gomer did not like staying at home, and often went into town to have some fun. But, once she had children, Gomer had to stay in the house all day to care for them. She found this very dull.

One day, Hosea returned to find his wife had left the family, and gone off with another man. In those days, if a wife was unfaithful, a man divorced her immediately. But the prophet was miserable without Gomer.

God spoke to Hosea. "Go and find your wife and bring her back," he said. "Forgive her for what she has done. The way you feel about Gomer is the way I feel about Israel. No matter how my people behave and worship other gods, I must love and protect them, and bring them back to me."

Hosea found Gomer, and used all his money to buy her back from the other man. Then the prophet took his beloved wife home. Now he understood exactly how God felt.

"Return to the Lord," Hosea preached to the people. "Ask him to forgive you for disobeying him. Those of you who are wise will realise that God's ways are best. The Lord loves you. If you obey him, he will save you from your enemies." Hosea warned everyone, "If you do not change, you are heading for destruction!"

But still the people of Israel did not listen.

Jonah and the Storm

Another prophet in Israel was a man called Jonah. One day, God spoke to Jonah. "Go to the great city of Nineveh and preach to the people," said God. "I want you to warn them to change their wicked ways, or I will destroy them."

Jonah could not believe that God was serious. Nineveh was the huge capital city of Assyria, and the Assyrian people had for a long time been powerful enemies of Israel. Why should he go and prophesy to foreigners? Why should God want to help these cruel people? Jonah thought they deserved all they got.

So, Jonah ignored what God had told him to do. In fact, he ran away. Instead of heading for Ninevah, Jonah boarded a ship heading in the opposite direction. It was bound for Tarshish in Spain. Jonah wanted to get as far from Assyria as he could.

The ship set sail, and Jonah went below deck to rest. Soon, the gentle movement of the waves rocked him off to sleep. But, after a while, the sky grew dark, and there was a terrible storm. A fierce wind blew the waves into walls of water which crashed down on the ship. The crew was terrified and called upon their gods to save them.

The captain rushed below deck to Jonah, to find him snoring away. "How can you sleep!" he shouted at the prophet, shaking him. "Pray to your god to save us! Maybe he will help us, and we won't all drown."

Then the sailors decided to draw lots to find out who was to blame for the disaster. They all wrote down their names, and one was picked out. It was Jonah's name. So, the sailors asked him, "Who are you? What have you done to cause us such trouble?"

Jonah told them he was a prophet. "I am from Israel," he said. "I worship the Lord, God of Heaven, the only true God who made the sea and the land." Jonah went on. "I have disobeyed God by running away from him. It's my fault this has happened to you. The best thing you can do is to throw me overboard."

But the captain would not hear of it. He was a good man, and he did not want to harm Jonah. Instead, the crew tried to row the ship back to land. But the storm grew even wilder. So, in the end, the captain prayed to God, "O Lord, do not blame us for killing an innocent man." Then, very reluctantly, he and the crew hurled Jonah overboard into the raging sea.

As soon as Jonah sank beneath the waves, the wind dropped and the sea grew calm again. The storm was over. The captain and crew fell on their knees and worshipped God, and thanked him for saving their lives.

Jonah and the Whale

But God was not going to let Jonah drown. He still had a job to do. As the prophet struggled about in the water, gasping for breath, a great whale appeared out of the depths of the sea and swallowed him up. For three days, Jonah stayed alive inside the dark, damp insides of the enormous fish. He knew that God had sent the whale to rescue him, and Jonah prayed to the Lord to thank him for saving his life.

The whale vomited Jonah up on to the seashore. At last, he was safely on dry land. Then God spoke again to Jonah. "Now will you go to Nineveh?" he asked. This time the prophet did as he was told.

When he reached Nineveh, Jonah was astonished. It was an enormous city with hundreds of thousands of people. The Assyrians were cruel and selfish, and worshipped many false gods. So, as the Lord had commanded, the prophet began to preach. "Turn from your wicked ways," he told the people, "or in forty days God will destroy your city." The people listened and took notice. The king listened, too.

Then the king ordered that the whole city should fast and pray, and ask God's forgiveness for the way they had behaved. Soon, everyone had started to live better lives. God saw what had happened, and he was pleased. He decided not to destroy the city after all.

But Jonah was not pleased. Although he had done his job, he did not understand why God had given these awful people a chance. Jonah would have preferred it if God had wiped them out. He was so angry and depressed, he lay on the ground. "I might as well be dead," Jonah said to God. Then he fell asleep in the sun.

God made a vine to grow up to give shade to Jonah, so he would not die of sunstroke. When he woke up, Jonah felt better, and was pleased to have the plant to give him shelter. But the next day, God sent a worm to chew the roots of the vine, so that it withered and died. Jonah was upset when the shady leaves disappeared.

Then God asked Jonah, "Why are you angry with me? You are unhappy about a dead vine that you did not water or cause to grow. So, why should I not care about people whom I created and love. They did not know about me until you came along. Why shouldn't I spare them, and their animals, from death?"

The Prophet Isaiah

While King Jeroboam II was king of Israel, the southern kingdom of Judah was ruled by King Uzziah. He loved and obeyed God, and when he died, the people wondered what would happen in Judah.

A young nobleman, called Isaiah, was concerned about what the future would hold, so he went to the temple to pray. While he was praying, he had a marvellous vision of God. Isaiah was so overcome by God's goodness that he was prepared to do anything the Lord asked of him. "Who will talk to my people?" asked God. "Who will be my messenger?"

"I'll go!" said Isaiah. "Send me."

So, God made Isaiah his prophet, and instructed him to try to turn the people from their wicked ways. God warned Isaiah that his job would not be easy, and that the people would not listen or understand. It would be a long time before they were ashamed of the way they lived and became holy again.

Despite this, Isaiah became a prophet of God. But, as the Lord had warned him, few people took notice of his words.

One man who should have listened to Isaiah, and obeyed, was King Ahaz of Judah. During his reign, the armies of Syria and Israel joined together to fight against the powerful Assyrians. They marched to Judah to force Ahaz to join their alliance, too.

King Ahaz was terrified, and asked Isaiah what God wanted him to do. "God tells you to keep calm and stand firm," said Isaiah. But the king did not listen. Although the prophet warned the king to obey, Ahaz panicked and asked Assyria for help. As a result, he brought a terrible disaster upon God's people.

The mighty Assyrians invaded Israel and captured its capital, Samaria. All the ten tribes of Israel were taken into exile, and never again returned to their homeland.

The people of Judah grieved for Israel. But Isaiah prophesied about a time in the future when there would be no more sadness and distress. Instead, there would be an everlasting peace. Although Galilee had just been crushed by the Assyrians, the Lord would send a saviour, who would be born in Galilee. Isaiah said, "For to us a child is born, to us a son is given, and he will be called Wonderful Counsellor, Mighty God, Everlasting Father, Prince of Peace. He will reign on David's throne for ever."

God hoped that Judah would learn a lesson from the appalling fate of Israel. For a while, they did.

The next king of Judah was a good man called Hezekiah. He loved God, and obeyed his laws. He cleared the temple of Assyrian gods, and brought the people back to worshipping the Lord. When they heard this, the cruel Assyrians marched to Jerusalem to teach Hezekiah a lesson.

Again, Isaiah was asked for God's advice. Once more, the prophet told the king to stand firm. "God will protect you," said Isaiah. "The enemy will go home without shooting a single arrow." This time, the king obeyed, and Jerusalem was saved.

The Prophet Jeremiah

After King Hezekiah of Judah died, his son, Manessah, became king. He did not obey God, nor did his son after him. However, the next king, Josiah, loved and obeyed the Lord.

King Josiah banned all the worship of Baal and the human sacrifices that had been taking place, and set about restoring and cleaning the temple. Buried under the clutter of idols that had been filling the temple, Josiah's workmen found a scroll. The high priest recognised it as a copy of God's law. When it was read out to the king, it became very clear to Josiah just how much the people of Israel had strayed from the way God wanted them to live. So, he ordered all the idols to be burned, and held a great feast at the time of the Passover.

But no matter what King Josiah ordered, or how much he loved God, the people he ruled did not have the same goodness in their hearts, and secretly continued in their old ways.

At this time in Judah, there was a young man called Jeremiah, who was training to be a priest. One day, God spoke to Jeremiah and asked him to be his prophet. "Please don't ask me to go out and speak to the people," said Jeremiah. "I am too young to be a prophet and I won't know what to say."

But God insisted. "Don't be afraid, Jeremiah," he said. "I will always be with you to protect you, and I will put my words into your mouth. You must warn my people that, unless they obey my law and stop their false worship, a great enemy will overpower them and Jerusalem will be destroyed."

Jeremiah could not think who this enemy would be, as Assyria had now lost its power. But he did as God had told him, and warned the people about what was in store. As usual, no one listened.

Then King Josiah was killed fighting against Egypt, and the Egyptians insisted that his weak son, Jehoiakim, should be king in his place. Jehoiakim had to do as the Egyptians told him, and this did not include obeying the Lord.

For twenty years, Jeremiah warned the people of Judah to obey God and turn from idol worship. But, still they took no notice. So, the Lord told Jeremiah to write down everything he had ever told the prophet on a large scroll.

"Now," said God. "Go to the temple and read the scroll to the people." So, as Jeremiah was banned from the temple, his helper, Baruch, took the scroll and read it aloud. Soon, news of this reached the king, and he ordered the scroll to be brought to him. Supporters of Jeremiah warned Baruch and him to hide from the king's anger. They knew Jehoiakim would be furious when he heard God's message read aloud. And he was.

After his secretary had read the contents of the scroll, the king snatched his penknife and slashed the scroll into pieces. Then he threw it on the fire and watched it burn. "Arrest Jeremiah!" ordered King Jehoiakim, but it was too late. The prophet and his helper were hidden away.

Then God spoke to Jeremiah. "Begin again," he said. "Take another scroll, and write it all out once more." God wanted to give his people every possible chance to change, so that their land could be saved from destruction.

The Destruction of Jerusalem

It soon became clear who the new powerful enemy of Judah was. The armies of King Nebuchadnezzar of Babylon had overcome those of Assyria and Egypt. As Egypt was under the control of Babylon, King Jehoiakim was forced to obey Nebuchadnezzar, too.

But, after a while, Jehoiakim began to plot against the king of Babylon, and that was a big mistake. Nebuchadnezzar decided it was time to attack Jerusalem.

By the time the armies of Babylon reached Jerusalem, Jehoiakim was dead. So, it was the new king who was taken captive, along with all the strongest, most clever citizens, and the most skilled workmen. Thousands of God's people were forced to march hundreds of miles to live in a foreign land, and the soldiers of Babylon stripped the temple of its treasures and carried them away.

Only the very weak were left behind in Jerusalem, and Nebuchadnezzar chose a new king, called Zedekiah, to rule over them. Jeremiah stayed in Jerusalem, and continued to preach to those that remained. Despite all that had happened to them, the people of Judah still did not turn back to God. The prophet warned Zedekiah that God wanted the king to obey Nebuchadnezzar, and that he was not to plot against him. "If you do this," said Jeremiah, "God says you will escape the terrible destruction that will come upon this land."

But Zedekiah and his advisers would not listen to the prophet. Jeremiah angered the king and his court so much that they beat him and put him in prison. Still God encouraged his prophet to call out his warnings.

The people of Jerusalem who were captives in Babylon had begun to learn their lesson, and were turning back to God's law. Jeremiah wrote to them, encouraging them to keep trusting God. "The Lord says that, after seventy years, he will bring you back from Babylon and restore everything to you. He will make a new law for you, to replace the one given to Moses. This new law will not be written down, but it will be in your hearts and minds. You will all know the Lord and be his people."

Meanwhile, Zedekiah continued to plot against Babylon. So, Nebuchadnezzar came back to punish the people of Judah. "Give in to Babylon," Jeremiah told the king, but even then he did not listen.

So, for two years, the city of Jerualem was besieged until the people starved. Then, the fierce warriors of Babylon broke into the city and pulled down its walls. They burned the temple, the palace and all the rich homes. They captured the king, and blinded him for his disobedience. Then, carrying with them all the treasures they could find, the soldiers of Nebuchadnezzar dragged the remaining citizens back to Babylon in chains.

Despite everything the Lord had done to save them, the people of Judah had continued to disobey God. Now they were forced to live in exile for many years.

Daniel and the Dream

The people of Judah who lived in exile in Babylon were called 'Jews' for short. The brightest and fittest of these Jews were selected and trained to serve in the court of the powerful King Nebuchadnezzar.

A young man, called Daniel, and his three friends, Shadrach, Meshach and Abednego, were among those chosen. These four Jews were men of God, and remained faithful to God's laws, so the Lord watched over them, and gave the men great knowledge. To Daniel, he also gave the gift of understanding visions and dreams. Nebuchadnezzar was very impressed with Daniel and his friends. Out of all his advisers they were the wisest.

One day, Nebuchadnezzar summoned all his magicians and astrologers. "I have had a strange dream," he said, "and I want to know what it means." The astrologers asked to be told the dream, so that they could interpret it. But the king would not reveal it to them. "I want you also to tell me what I dreamt, as well as its meaning!" he boomed.

"Your majesty," they said. "No man on earth can do what you ask." When he heard this, Nebuchadnezzar was so furious he ordered for all his advisers to be executed immediately. This also included the four Jews.

The night before the execution, Daniel and the others prayed that God would reveal the dream and its meaning. Sure enough, during the night God told Daniel all that he needed to know.

So, the next morning, Daniel asked to be taken to the king.

"Well," said Nebuchadnezzar, "are you able to tell me all about my dream?"

"Your majesty," replied Daniel, "no wise man could ever do what you ask, but there is a God in heaven who explains such mysteries. He has told me your dream."

Daniel went on, "In your dream you saw a large statue of a man. The head was made of pure gold, the chest and arms were silver, the thighs were bronze and the legs were iron. But the feet of the statue were iron mixed with clay. As you were gazing at the statue, a great boulder came rolling towards it. The rock crashed on to the feet of clay and smashed them. Then the statue crumbled into dust, and was scattered in the wind. But the boulder became a huge mountain and filled the whole earth."

The king was amazed. "Yes," he said, "you're right! But what does it mean?"

So, Daniel revealed what God had told him. "The statue represents all the empires of the world. At the top is yours, the richest and most powerful of all. Then there are others that will come, which will be less mighty. But no matter how strong, these kingdoms will not last. The simple boulder that destroys the statue is the kingdom that God will create. It will grow greater and greater until it fills the whole world."

Nebuchadnezzar was astonished at what he heard. "Your God is surely the greatest of all," he said, "for you were the only one able to interpret such a mystery."

The Fiery Furnace

King Nebuchadnezzar was so delighted with Daniel that he made him chief of all his advisers, and gave him many rich presents.

The king often thought about the meaning of his dream but, instead of remembering about God, he thought more and more about the statue. He got so carried away with his own importance that he ordered his craftsmen to create a gigantic gold statue of himself.

When it was finished, the huge statue of the king was erected in the province of Babylon, and a great unveiling ceremony was organised. As well as summoning the ordinary people, Nebuchadnezzar invited all the important officials of his kingdom, including Daniel's three friends, Shadrach, Meshach and Abednego.

Once everyone was assembled in front of the great statue, a herald issued a proclamation to the people. "This is what you are commanded to do. As soon as you hear the band start to play the royal music, you must fall down and worship the golden image of Nebuchadnezzar. Anyone who does not worship the statue will be thrown into a blazing furnace."

Then the band started to play and all the thousands of people that were gathered fell to the ground and worshipped the statue. All, that is, except three. Shadrach, Meshach and Abednego could not worship anything other than God.

When the king heard about this, he ordered the three Jews to be brought before him. "Is it true that you did not bow down and worship my golden image?" he said. "Do you realise that you will be thrown into a blazing furnace?"

Nebuchadnezzar gave the young men another chance to do as he ordered. But they told him, "We can never worship anyone other than God. If you throw us into the furnace, then our God is able to rescue us from the flames. Even if he doesn't, we must still worship him."

The king was enraged by these words, and ordered that the furnace should be made as hot as possible. When it was white hot, he gave orders for the three Jews to be tied up and thrown in. The heat of the furnace was so intense, the soldiers who threw the prisoners in were scorched to death at the entrance.

From a safe distance, Nebuchadnezzar peered into the raging flames. Then he leapt to his feet in amazement. "Weren't there only three men thrown into the fire?" he asked his officials. They assured him that this was so. "Look!" he said, pointing. "I see four men walking in the flames. The fourth looks like an angel of God."

The king shouted into the furnace, and ordered Shadrach, Meshach and Abednego to come out. Nebuchadnezzar and his officials stared in disbelief when they saw the three Jews. Not a hair on their heads was singed, their clothes were not scorched and their bodies had not been harmed in any way.

"Praise the God of Shadrach, Meshach and Abednego," said the king. "He delivered them from the flames. No one is to say a word against this God ever again."

The Madness of Nebuchadnezzar

K ing Nebuchadnezzar continued to rule his great empire successfully for many years to come. Nothing troubled him until, one night, he had another strange dream.

As usual, the king summoned his magicians and astrologers to interpret the dream, but none of them could explain it at all.

So, Nebuchadnezzar sent for Daniel. "I know that the spirit of God is in you," he said, "and that no mystery is too difficult for you to explain. Please help me to understand this dream." Daniel listened carefully as the king described what he had seen.

"I saw an enormous tree which grew so large that its top reached the sky, and everyone in the world could see it. The tree had beautiful leaves and luscious fruit, and it provided food and shelter for all the birds and animals around. Then, suddenly, an angel from heaven flew down and called out, 'Cut down the tree and trim its branches. Strip off its leaves and scatter its fruit. But leave the stump in the ground.' "

Nebuchadnezzar went on, "Then the tree stump turned into a man. The angel said, 'This man will live in the wild like an animal and, for seven years, his mind will become like that of an animal, too. This is to show everyone in the world that God rules over even the mightiest of men.' "

Daniel was very worried when he heard what his king had dreamed. For a while, he did not speak. "Daniel," said Nebuchadnezzar, "do not be afraid to tell me what you think."

Reluctantly, Daniel explained the meaning of the dream. "The enormous tree that you saw is you, your majesty," he said. "You have become strong and powerful. But, unless you recognise that God is greater than you, he will take away your power. You will lose your mind and live in the wild, away from your people and everything you know. Your kingdom will only be restored to you when you have learned that only God rules the world."

Then Daniel begged the king, "Please, your majesty, take notice of this dream. Be kind to the poor and needy, and humble yourself before God. In this way, you may avoid disaster."

The king listened, but soon forgot Daniel's words. A year later, as he stood on his palace roof in Babylon, he looked out at the city stretched before him and said to himself, "What a magnificent city I have built. How clever and powerful I am!"

As soon as the words were spoken, the king was immediately overcome by a terrible madness. He did not know who he was, and he lived like an animal, eating grass and plants out in the wild. His hair grew long and matted, and his nails were like claws. For a long time, Nebuchadnezzar lived like this until, one day, his mind cleared and he became sane again. It was then he realized that he owed everything to God, and that only the Lord was truly powerful.

Once the king had learned his lesson, his kingdom and riches were restored to him, and he lived the rest of his life worshipping and praising God.

Daniel and the New Law

Many years later, a young king called Belshazzar ruled Babylon. One night, he gave a great banquet for his court, at which everyone became very drunk and rowdy. In his drunken haze, Belshazzar shocked his guests by sending for the golden cups that had been brought from the temple in Jerusalem. The king and his wives then used the sacred cups to drink to their own false gods.

God was so angry with Belshazzar that he wrote a message of doom on the wall in front of the king. Daniel explained to the terrified young man that the writing foretold the loss of his kingdom. And this is exactly what happened. Babylon was soon overrun by a new powerful enemy. The combined armies of the Medes and the Persians captured the city, and their king, Darius, took over the throne.

King Darius was the ruler of a vast empire, so he appointed one hundred and twenty officials to help control the provinces. In charge of the officials were three administrators, the chief of which was Daniel. Darius was a strong and wise king, and he had soon discovered that Daniel was the most clever and trustworthy man at court.

Some of the other officials and administrators were bitterly jealous of Daniel, and looked for a way to make him unpopular with the king. "The only way to be rid of him," one said, "is to find something about his Jewish religion that could get him into trouble."

Everyone knew that, three times a day, Daniel knelt and prayed to God. They also knew that nothing would prevent him from worshipping the Lord. So, Daniel's enemies thought of a plan.

"Your majesty," they said to King Darius. "All the officials and administrators have decided that it would be advisable if you were to issue a new law. This states that anyone who wants to ask for anything at all during the next thirty days should only do so by consulting you. If anyone makes their request to another man or god, they are to be thrown into the lion's den."

Darius thought this law would emphasise his supreme power, so he agreed to it and signed the document. He did not realise that it would be a trap for his devoted servant.

When Daniel heard about the new law, he guessed what his enemies were up to. But there was nothing he could do. As usual, three times a day, he knelt down to pray. The officials spied on Daniel, and saw he was disobeying the law. They went to Darius and told him they had found someone who was disregarding his orders.

"Your majesty," they said. "Daniel pays no attention to the law that you have signed. He prays to his God three times a day." When Darius heard this, he realised that he had walked straight into their trap. He trusted Daniel more than anyone else, and now he had to sentence him to death. The king tried to think of a way to rescue his friend, but he had no choice. He had agreed to the law and now he must carry it out.

"Daniel," said Darius gravely, "may your God, whom you worship, rescue you from the lions."

Daniel in the Lions' Den

Then King Darius gave orders for his chief servant to be thrown into the pit full of fierce, hungry wild beasts. A huge stone was rolled over the entrance to the den, so there was no way of escape.

The king was so unhappy at what he had done, he went straight to bed without food or drink. Then he tossed and turned all night long, unable to sleep a wink. At dawn, Darius leapt out of bed and rushed to the lion's den to see what had happened.

He called out, "Daniel, servant of the living God, has your God whom you serve saved you from the lions?"

From the darkness below, a voice answered clearly, "Your majesty, my God sent an angel to shut the mouths of the lions. They have not harmed me because I am innocent and have not wronged your majesty in any way."

"Get him out of there!" ordered the delighted king. When he examined Daniel, he found no trace of any wound. Daniel had trusted God, and the Lord had protected him.

King Darius was furious with the officials who had trapped both him and his servant, Daniel. He pointed at the ringleaders. "Now throw *them* to the lions!" he ordered.

Then the king issued a new proclamation. It said, "I issue a decree that in every part of my kingdom people must worship and respect the God of Daniel. He performs great signs and wonders. He rescued Daniel from the lions."

The Prophet Ezekiel

When Nebuchadnezzar had first invaded Jerusalem and taken its stronger citizens into exile, there was amongst them a young man called Ezekiel. Like Jeremiah, Ezekiel had been training to be a priest in the temple of Jerusalem. Now that he was an exile in Babylon, God called him to be his prophet.

At the age of thirty, Ezekiel had an incredible vision of God. He saw the Lord seated on a throne in a scene of dazzling brightness and colour. God's great goodness and radiance shone out so strongly that it made Ezekiel even more aware of how wrong his people were to disobey him. The Lord wanted Ezekiel to encourage the Jews in exile to turn back to him and obey his laws. Ezekiel was also to warn the people about the destruction of Jerusalem that was soon to take place.

Ezekiel told the Jews what was going to happen in the future by his actions, rather than by his words. One day, he sat down in the marketplace and drew a picture of Jerusalem on a brick. Around the brick, he made models of armies in the sand. The next day, as the other Jews watched him, Ezekiel measured out a small amount of flour, and made a tiny loaf of bread.

Every day this was all he ate, and all he drank were two cupfuls of water. As Ezekiel grew thinner and thinner, the people realised what this meant. The citizens of Jerusalem would starve as their city was besieged.

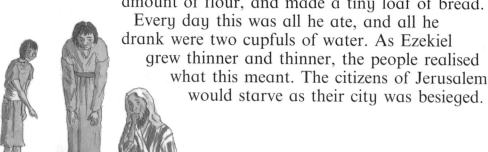

Then the prophet cut off his hair and beard, and divided it into three sections. The first he burnt, the second he chopped up with his sword, and the third he scattered in the wind. But Ezekiel ran to gather up some of the hairs that had been scattered, and wrapped them gently in his cloak. The Jews could see that the hair represented their nation. Although a terrible disaster was going to happen, God would rescue some of his people and bring them back to him.

As well as a warning, God also wanted Ezekiel to give the people a message of hope. So, the prophet had another vision, the meaning of which he was to tell to the Jews.

In this vision, Ezekiel was in a valley. The ground was covered in thousands of dry human bones. God asked Ezekiel to tell the bones that the Lord wanted them to come to life again. The prophet did as he was told. As Ezekiel watched, the bones began to join together. Muscles, flesh and skin grew on them until, lying on the ground, were many lifeless people.

Then God said, "Ezekiel, order the wind to blow breath into these bodies." So, again, Ezekiel did as God commanded. Gradually, the lifeless people began to move. Then they stood up and became a vast army. After that, the vision faded away.

"Ezekiel," said God, "these bones are the people of Israel who have given up hope of returning home. But I am still their God, and I will give their land back to them. They will have a new beginning and a new life."

Nehemiah

After the Jews had been in exile in Babylon for seventy years, at last they were given the opportunity to return to their homeland. King Cyrus of Persia, who now ruled Babylon, issued a proclamation to the Jews: "Go back home and rebuild the temple in Jerusalem. Those who are poor must be given enough money and supplies to make the journey, too." The king gave back all the treasures from the temple which Nebuchadnezzar had stolen. Then he sent them on their way.

The Jews joyfully made the long journey back to Judea. But, when they arrived, they looked in horror at what remained of their great city and the beautiful temple of Solomon. There was nothing but piles of rubble and broken remains. What a job they had ahead of them!

Although they worked very hard, the Jews were overwhelmed at the amount of rebuilding they had to do. Also, they were constantly being hampered by the Samaritans, an unfriendly race of people who now lived nearby. They did not want Jerusalem to be powerful again, and did everything possible to stop the building work. After many years of struggle, the temple was finally finished. There was great celebration and praise as the new temple was dedicated to God.

Seventy years later, however, the rebuilding of Jerusalem still was not finished. The huge task of reconstructing the walls and making the city gates remained.

Reports of this reached the Jews who remained in Babylon, one of whom was a great man of God, called Nehemiah.

Nehemiah was the wine steward to the Emperor Artaxerxes. It was his job to taste the king's wine in case it was poisoned. One day, the Emperor noticed that his wine steward was very depressed, and he asked him the reason why. Nehemiah had been praying to God for an opportunity to speak to the king, so he said, "Your majesty, I am sad because the city of my people still lies in ruins." Then he paused, and asked, "If it please the king, I would like to go to Jerusalem and help with the rebuilding."

The Emperor gave Nehemiah leave to go home. He also gave him money and wood from the royal forest to make the city gates. Then, with an escort of soldiers to protect him on his journey, Nehemiah travelled to Jerusalem.

Nehemiah was amazed when he saw just how much there was to be done. But he encouraged the people, and divided them into family groups, giving each group a part of the wall to build. When the dreaded Samaritans threatened to attack again, Nehemiah instructed the Jews to arm themselves with swords. Then they carried on rebuilding, armed ready for battle. After working night and day for a long time, the work was completed, and Jerusalem was safe.

All the Jews gathered together to hear Ezra read out God's law. They listened hard and promised that this time they would learn from their mistakes, trust in God and obey him.

Esther Becomes Queen

Between the time of the rebuilding of the temple in Jerusalem and the time of Nehemiah, there was a king of Persia named Xerxes. He ruled over the great Persian empire, which included Babylonia. Xerxes was a moody, unpredictable man. Like all eastern kings at that time, he had a huge harem with many wives. But among these he had only one queen, the beautiful Queen Vashti.

Unfortunately, Queen Vashti offended Xerxes in the third year of his reign. As a result, the emperor banished her from his kingdom.

The king's ministers suggested that he find a new queen. "Let a search be made for beautiful young girls throughout the land," they said. "The king can choose a new queen from these." The emperor liked this idea. So all the prettiest girls were brought to the palace to be presented to the king.

Among those chosen was a beautiful Jewish girl named Esther. She was an orphan and had been adopted by her cousin, Mordecai. He was one of the Jews who still lived in Babylon.

Mordecai escorted Esther to the palace and was given a job there, so that as her guardian, he could watch over her. Mordecai advised his cousin not to tell anyone that she was Jewish.

When finally the lovely young girls were presented to the emperor, Esther was the one whom he found to be the most attractive in every way. "You shall be my queen!" said Xerxes. And then he gave a great banquet for his beautiful new bride.

The Plot against the Jews

While he was working in the palace, Mordecai overheard two of the king's officers plotting to kill the Emperor. So, Mordecai quickly told his cousin, the queen, to warn her husband. This she did, and the two plotters were executed. All these events were written down in the royal records.

Not long afterwards, the king promoted a man called Haman to be his prime minister. All the officials and nobles bowed to Haman as he walked by. Everyone, that is, except Mordecai.

Haman was a proud, scheming, ambitious man. When it came to his notice that Mordecai, the Jew, did not show him respect, Haman was furious. He decided that not only did he want to kill Mordecai, but he would kill *all* the Jews in the kingdom of Persia.

Haman consulted with the court astrologers, who cast lots to choose the best day to eliminate the Jews. The lot, known as the 'pur', fell on the twelfth month. This was to be the time.

Then Haman went to the Emperor. "Your majesty," he said, "there is a race of people in your land whose customs are different from ours, and who do not obey the king's laws. If it pleases the king, let an order be given to destroy them. I will pay into the treasury a large sum of money to pay the men that carry out this business." Haman intended to steal the Jews' own silver to pay for this.

Without thinking, the Emperor took his signet ring and put his seal to the new law. So, it was announced that on the allotted day, every single Jew in the empire would be murdered.

When Mordecai heard this terrible news, he was horrified. He sent a message to Esther. "You must go to the king," he wrote. "Plead mercy for the Jews."

But Esther was frightened. The Emperor had not asked to see her for a month. To enter the royal presence without the king's request could mean the death sentence. "I dare not go to him," replied Esther, "he may no longer be pleased with me."

But Mordecai insisted. "You are a Jew. You will die anyway if this law is enforced. Perhaps the reason God has given you such a privileged position is in order to save his people." So, Esther asked Mordecai and all the other Jews to fast and pray for three days. "Then I will go to the king," she said. "If I die, so be it."

Three days later, the queen put on her finest royal robes and jewels. Then, summoning all her courage, she went to the doorway of the Emperor's throne room. If he was in a good mood, he would hold out his golden sceptre, summoning her into his presence. In a bad mood, he may order her execution.

The king looked at his beautiful wife. Then, slowly, he held out his golden sceptre. "What is your request, Queen Esther?" he asked. Esther asked the king if he and his prime minister would dine with her that evening. The king agreed and later that evening the queen served a banquet to Haman and her husband.

"What would you like me to do?" asked the king. "Whatever your request, it will be granted." So, Esther delayed a little longer, and asked the king if he and Haman would again dine with her the following night.

Esther saves the Jews

The prime minster returned home feeling very pleased with himself. "The Queen has asked me to dine *again*!" he told his wife. "I must have impressed her. But I will not be happy until Mordecai is dead." His wife suggested that Haman build a gallows and hang Mordecai. "What a good idea!" said the prime minister. "I'll do it tomorrow."

Meanwhile, that night the Emperor could not sleep. While he was awake, he called for his secretary to read him the royal record of events. Amongst these were the details of the plot to murder him. So, the Emperor was reminded that Mordecai had saved his life.

"Was that man rewarded in any way?" he asked his secretary.

"No, your majesty," the secretary replied.

At that moment, Haman came to seek an audience with the king. He was planning to request the execution of Mordecai. As he was ushered into the Emperor's presence, Xerxes asked Haman, "What would you do for someone you wanted to honour?"

Haman stopped in his tracks, and thought that the king wanted to reward him. So, he replied, "Dress him in a royal robe and place him on a royal horse, with a royal crest. Let the man be led through the city proclaiming, 'This is what is done for a man the king honours!' "

"Go at once!" ordered the king. "Do this for Mordecai." Haman was horrified when he heard these words. Obviously he could not now request Mordecai's death.

That night, Haman and the Emperor dined with Queen Esther. Afterwards, the king asked the queen, "Now, what is your request? It will be given to you."

Esther took a deep breath and asked, "Your majesty, please spare my life and that of my people, for we have been condemned to death."

"What!" cried Xerxes. "What man would dare to do such a thing?"

Esther pointed at Haman. "That man," she said. "That vile Haman!"

The king knew he had been tricked by Haman, and he was furious. He paced up and down the garden, thinking of what to do.

Then a loyal servant said, "Your majesty, Haman has built a gallows near his house. It is to hang Mordecai, who spoke up to help the king."

"Then hang Haman on it!" boomed the Emperor. So, the soldiers took the prime minister away to his death.

The Persian Emperor, however, could not change any law once he had put his seal on it. He could not cancel the order to murder the Jews. What he did do was issue a proclamation throughout the land that on the day allotted to the execution, the Jews were to arm themselves and fight those who came to kill them. This they did.

The Jews have never forgotten the day Esther risked her life to save them. To celebrate the anniversary of Purim (the day chosen for the mass execution) religious Jews always read out the book of Esther, and thank God for their deliverance.

The New Testament

This part of the Bible is called the New Testament because God made a *new* promise. He sent his own son, Jesus, into the world to offer forgiveness and a new life to those who believe and trust in him. The New Testament is about Jesus – his life, his teaching and his healing. It was written by the followers that Jesus chose and trusted.

Mediterranean
Sea

 Tyre

Mount
Hermon

Caesarea Philippi

Capernaum Bethsaida

Sea of
Galilee

Cana
Nazareth

GALILEE

Caesarea

Samaria

River Jordan

Jericho

Joppa

ARABIAN
DESERT

Jerusalem • Bethphage
Bethlehem • Caesarea

JUDEA

Dead
Sea

Gaza

ISRAEL

Masada •

171

The Birth of John the Baptist

Four centuries after the last of the Old Testament prophets, the Jewish people were once again under the control of a powerful enemy, the Romans. They had conquered Canaan, and given it the Roman name, Palestine. Judea was now a tiny part of the huge Roman Empire. Roman troops occupied the land, and the Jews had to pay taxes to the Roman Emperor, Augustus. The Jewish people longed for freedom, and wanted a saviour or a king, like David, to rescue them from their troubles.

The king of the Jews at this time was Herod. The Emperor, Augustus, let Herod rule over Palestine on his behalf. In return, Herod had to keep the Jews tightly under control.

The Jews prayed to God to send them a king who would save them. Every day a priest, called Zechariah, asked the Lord to help the Jewish people. Zechariah was a good man. He and his wife, Elizabeth, loved and obeyed God. They were sad because, although they had been married for a long time, they had never had a child.

One day, it was Zechariah's turn to be the priest to burn the incense on the altar of the holy temple. After he had done this, he was to come out and bless the crowds of people who were worshipping there. Zechariah entered the sacred inner sanctuary to burn the incense, and again prayed to God to send a king who would save the Jews.

Suddenly, an angel appeared beside the altar. Zechariah was terrified. "Don't be afraid," said the angel. "God has heard your prayers. Your wife, Elizabeth, will have a son, and you will call him John. He will be a great prophet of God, and he will prepare the people for the coming of the Lord, who is God's promised King."

Zechariah was stunned. "How can this be?" he asked. "My wife and I are now old."

"I am Gabriel," said the angel. "God has sent me to tell you these things. Because you have not believed, you will not speak again until the day all this happens."

Zechariah staggered out to where the people were waiting, but he could only bless them with signs as he could not talk. The crowds realised that something very special had happened.

"He must have seen a vision!" they gasped.

Then Zechariah returned home to Elizabeth, where he wrote down everything that had happened. "How the Lord has blessed me," said Elizabeth. "At last, I am to have a child."

Nine months later, Elizabeth gave birth to a son. All their relatives came to visit the baby. They asked Elizabeth if he was to be called Zechariah, after his father, but Elizabeth replied that he was to be called John. The relatives were surprised and looked at Zechariah. So, the priest wrote down, "His name is John."

As soon as he had written the name, Zechariah was able to speak. He was filled with joy and sang, "Let us thank God. He has remembered his people and is sending a saviour. This child will be the prophet who will prepare the way."

Mary, Joseph and the Angel

North of Judea, in a place called Galilee, there was a town called Nazareth. Here lived a fine man called Joseph. He was a descendant of the great King David. Joseph was a carpenter and worked hard for a living. He was happy as he was going to marry a kind and gentle girl called Mary.

One day, when Mary was sitting quietly alone in her house, a bright light filled the room, and she heard a voice. Mary looked up. There, in front of her, was God's angel, Gabriel.

"Do not be afraid," said Gabriel. "God is pleased with you. He has sent me to you with good news. You are going to have a very special son, and you must call him Jesus. He will be God's promised King. He is the one everyone is waiting for. His kingdom will never end."

"How can I have a baby?" asked Mary. "I am not yet married."

"This is something that God will do," said Gabriel. "The baby will be God's own Son. Your cousin, Elizabeth, is having a baby, too. She thought she would never have children. You see, nothing is too hard for God."

"I don't understand," said Mary. "But I will do whatever God wants."

When the angel had gone, Mary sat and
thought for a while. Then she decided to go and
visit her cousin Elizabeth, who was pregnant,
too. Elizabeth was very pleased to see Mary.
They hugged and kissed each other in joy.

"Isn't it wonderful!" said Elizabeth. "How
happy you must be, Mary. You are going to be
the mother of my Lord."

Mary was happy. She stayed with Elizabeth
for three months and then returned home.

But when Mary told the news of the baby to
Joseph, he was puzzled and upset. He could not
believe what Mary was telling him. It seemed
very strange to him that an angel of God could
have appeared to Mary. Joseph decided that if
she was having a baby he could not marry
Mary after all.

But, that night, Joseph had a dream. In the
dream, one of God's angels spoke to Joseph.
"Don't be afraid to marry Mary," said the
angel. "She has done nothing wrong. God has
chosen Mary to be the mother of his Son – the
promised Lord. You must call him Jesus, which
means 'the one who saves'. He is going to save
his people from their sins. You must marry
Mary, and look after Jesus as if he were your
own son."

The next morning, Joseph felt much better.
He realised that Mary had told him the truth.
Joseph quickly went to see her. "I'm sorry I did
not believe you, Mary," he said. "We must get
married straight away."

The Birth of Jesus

Mary and Joseph were married, and lived happily together in Nazareth, waiting for the birth of the baby. One day, the Emperor Augustus issued a new law. He wanted to know how many people were in his empire, so they could all pay him taxes. He ordered every man to return to the town of his birth, and put his name on a register. This new law was written down and sent to all parts of the Roman Empire.

Soon, the news reached Nazareth. "My family comes from Bethlehem," Joseph told Mary. "We will have to go there to register our names."

Bethlehem was far away from Nazareth, in the hills of Judea. Although it was nearly time for the baby to be born, Mary and Joseph had to obey the law, and make the long journey south.

They journeyed for many days along the hot, dusty road. Each night, they slept out in the open under the cold, dark sky. At last, they came to Judea. "Tomorrow we will reach Bethlehem," Joseph told Mary. "And there we will find an inn for you to rest in comfort."

The next day, Mary and Joseph set off on the final stage of their journey. Late in the day, feeling very tired and weary, they reached the little town of Bethlehem. It was very crowded as many others had also come to register.

Mary felt hot and uncomfortable. She knew it was almost time for her baby to be born. "We must find somewhere to stay, Joseph," she said. But everywhere they tried was full. Joseph knocked on the door of another inn.

"Sorry, we've no room here," said the innkeeper. "Everywhere in town is the same. You won't find anywhere to stay now."

"My wife is about to have her baby," said Joseph anxiously. But the innkeeper shook his head sadly.

Then someone took pity on Mary and thought of a place they could stay. It was a cave where animals were kept. The stable was dirty and smelly and full of hay, but at least it was somewhere to shelter for the night.

Mary and Joseph went into the warm stable, and Mary lay down on the hay to rest. And there, among the dirt and the animals, her baby was born. Mary wrapped him up warmly and, as there was no cradle, she laid him in the manger to sleep.

Mary and Joseph gazed in wonder at the tiny baby. As the angel Gabriel had told them, they called him Jesus. "This is God's promised King," said Joseph. "He has come to save us."

The Shepherds' Story

On the hillside outside Bethlehem, there were shepherds watching over their flocks of sheep. They looked down on the sleeping town, and were glad to be away from the crowds, in the peace and quiet of the hills.

Suddenly, an incredible brightness lit up the dark sky. "What's that?" cried a shepherd. They all looked up in wonder and amazement. There, shining above them was an angel of God. The shepherds were terrified.

"Don't be afraid," said the angel. "I have come to tell you good news which will bring joy to all the world. Today, in Bethlehem, a baby was born. He is the Saviour – God's promised King. Go and see him. You will find the baby wrapped up warmly, lying in a manger."

Then, all at once, the whole sky was full of angels. They were singing together, praising and thanking God for his gift to the world.

"Glory to God in heaven," they sang, "and peace on earth to those who love him."

The shepherds could not believe their eyes. Then, just as suddenly as they had come, the angels disappeared. The sky was dark again, and everything was quiet. "Come on, let's go to Bethlehem," said one shepherd. "We must find out what this is all about."

So, the shepherds set off across the fields and made their way into the town.

"The angel said the baby was in a manger,"
they whispered among themselves. "He must
have been born in a stable somewhere."

The shepherds moved quietly through
Bethlehem, looking in every stable they could
find. Finally, tucked away behind an inn, they
found the cave. "The innkeeper sometimes puts
his animals in there," said one of the shepherds.
"Let's have a look."

The shepherds peeped into the stable. Sitting
quietly on the hay, among all the animals, they
saw Mary and Joseph. And there, lying in the
manger, was a tiny, newborn baby boy. Just as
the angel had said, the baby was wrapped up to
keep him safe and warm in the cold, night air.

As soon as they saw the child, the shepherds
knelt down and worshipped him. "We saw an
angel in the sky," they said. "He told us that
this baby will bring great joy to all the world.
He is the Saviour we have been waiting for."

Then the shepherds told Mary and Joseph
everything that had happened that night, out
on the dark hillside. Mary listened carefully to
what the shepherds said. She knew she would
never forget all the wonderful things that the
angel had told them.

The shepherds returned to their sheep on
the hillside. They were overjoyed that God
had sent an angel to speak to them. As
they ran through the fields, they sang
hymns of praise for all that had happened.

The Wise Men visit King Herod

Meanwhile, in distant lands a long way to the East, there were others who also hoped for the birth of a new king. Wise men, called astronomers, studied the stars and planets looking for signs in the sky that might show that something unusual was going to happen.

One night, a very bright star shone in the sky. "Look," said one of the wise men. "There's a new star. I've never seen that one before. It's shining more brightly than any of the others. I wonder what it can mean?" The astronomers looked in their scrolls to find out if the bright star was a sign of something special.

"Such a star may mean that a great king has been born," said one of the wise men. "Perhaps it is the promised King we've all been waiting for. We must follow the star and find out."

The wise men loaded up their camels and set off towards the land over which the star seemed to shine. They carried with them rich presents, ready to give to the new king.

The astronomers travelled for a long time until at last, tired and weary, they came to the land of Israel. "We must go to Jerusalem," said one of the wise men. "The king's palace will be in that city." So, they made their way to the palace to search for the newborn king.

When they reached the palace, they met King
Herod. He was a greedy and jealous man, who
ruled over the land of Israel by order of the
mighty Roman Emperor. The wise men told
King Herod why they had come. When he
heard about a new king, Herod was secretly
very angry and upset. He did not want anyone
to take away his power. But Herod did not
show the wise men he was worried. Instead,
he pretended to be pleased. He wanted the
astronomers to find the new king so that he
could kill him.

Herod knew of an ancient prophesy that a
special king would be born in the town of
Bethlehem. "Go on with your search," he said
to the wise men. "Go to Bethlehem. And when
you find the new king, come and tell me where
he is, so that I can take him presents, too."

The Wise Men visit Jesus

So the wise men followed the star until they came to the town of Bethlehem. The star was shining right above it. That night, the astronomers searched the town for the child, and they came to a place where the star was directly overhead. The wise men knocked gently on the door and entered. It was poor and simple – not at all like the rich palace they had expected. There were Joseph and Mary, with Jesus cradled in Mary's arms.

When they saw the child, the wise men knelt down and worshipped him. "At last," they said, "we have found the Promised One, the newborn King." They gave the baby their rich gifts of gold, frankincense and myrrh.

Afterwards, the wise men left the little family in peace, and rested for a while before their long journey home to the East.

That night, as they slept, God warned the wise men not to return to Herod. So, the next day, the astronomers chose a different route home. They set off to their lands in the East, rejoicing that they had seen the King.

The Escape into Egypt

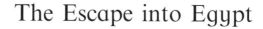

The same night that God warned the wise men, he also spoke to Joseph in a dream. "Get up," he said. "Take the child and his mother, and escape into Egypt. Stay there until I tell you. Herod is going to search for the child to kill him."

So, in the middle of the night, Joseph got up and woke Mary. Then, under cover of darkness, they quickly set off on their journey.

Meanwhile, Herod waited impatiently for the wise men to return to Jerusalem to tell him exactly where the newborn king was to be found. As the months went by, he realised that the wise men had outwitted him. The king was furious. Although he was now an old man, Herod was determined to eliminate any threat to his power. He had to think of a way to kill this baby king.

It was now over a year since the wise men had told Herod they had first seen the star. Therefore, there was only one way to be sure of killing his enemy.

Mad with rage, King Herod issued a terrible command. "Go to Bethlehem and the areas all around," he said to his soldiers. "Kill every boy under the age of two!"

The soldiers did as the king had ordered, and there was terrible grief and suffering in the land. Of course, Herod did not know that the child he sought was by now safely in Egypt, out of harm's way.

Not long after this time of terrible cruelty, King Herod died. Once more, an angel appeared to Joseph in a dream.

"Get up," he said. "Take your child and his mother back to Israel. Those who were trying to harm the child are dead."

Joseph, Mary and Jesus journeyed back to Israel. But when they came near to Bethlehem, they heard that Herod's evil son was now king. He was ruling only the south of Israel, so Joseph thought it would be safer to go north.

So, instead of going to Bethlehem, Mary and Joseph went north to Galilee. Once again, they settled in Nazareth, and lived there happily with Jesus.

The Boy Jesus

Each year in the spring, a great festival took place in Jerusalem. This was to celebrate the Passover, the time when the children of Israel had escaped from slavery in Egypt, years earlier.

When Jesus was twelve years old, Mary and Joseph made the long journey to the city to join in the festivities. Jews from all over Palestine came to Jerusalem, and it was crowded with people meeting friends and relatives they had not seen for a year. The Passover Feast lasted for a week, and when it was over the visitors once again set off for home.

Mary and Joseph travelled with many other families. The women walked along together with the young children, and the men and the older boys followed on behind.

After they had been travelling for a day, Joseph caught up with Mary. "Where's Jesus?" he asked. Mary froze in panic.

"I thought he was with you!" she answered. "He's twelve now, and too old to be with these little children."

But Jesus was nowhere to be seen. None of the other families had seen him either. "We'll have to go back to the city," said Joseph. So, he and Mary started the long trek back.

For three days, they searched Jerusalem. No one had seen Jesus. Mary and Joseph were tired and weary with anxiety.

Finally, they found Jesus in the temple. There he was, sitting calmly amongst the priests and teachers, listening to their teaching and asking questions. Everyone was amazed at his knowledge and understanding.

"Jesus! How could you do this to us?" asked
Mary. "We've been very worried. We've been
looking everywhere for you." His mother was
relieved to find him, but she was angry and
upset as well.

Jesus seemed to be surprised that he had
caused his parents such worry. "Why were you
searching?" he said gently. "I thought you
would realise that I must be in my Father's
house." Mary and Joseph were so astonished
and glad to find their son, they said no more.

The family returned to Nazareth, where Jesus
grew up into a fine, wise, young man. He
always obeyed his parents and everyone loved
him. But Mary never forgot what had happened
that spring. She knew her son was special, and
she wondered what was going to happen next.

Jesus is baptized

The years went by, and both Jesus and his cousin, John, grew into men. As had been foretold by his father, Zechariah, John became a prophet of God. Just as Elijah had done, John went to live in the wild, living off honey and locusts in the desert.

John travelled around the area near the River Jordan, preaching to the people. "Listen all of you," he said. "God's kingdom is coming. You must change your lives and obey God's laws." He told those who listened that if they were sorry for the wrong things they had done they could be 'baptized', or washed clean of their sins, and that God would forgive them.

"What should we do then?" the crowd asked.

John taught the people to be honest, generous and kind to each other. "Be content with what you have," said John. "Share your food and belongings with those who have none." Many people listened to John's words, and he baptized them in the River Jordan.

Some of the Jews thought that perhaps this man of God was the promised saviour that they had been waiting for.

But John told them, "I baptize you with water, but I am preparing you for a very important person. Someone much greater than I will come, whose sandals I am not worthy enough to unfasten. He will baptize you with God's power. He is the promised King that you are all waiting for."

One day, Jesus came to the Jordan and saw his cousin, John, baptizing the people. He went up to the prophet and asked if he could also be baptized. But John was amazed and felt unworthy of this.

"You have always obeyed God," he said. "You have nothing to be sorry for. You are a better person than I. It would be better for you to baptize me."

But Jesus answered, "I believe God wants you to do this."

So, John agreed. Jesus went into the shallows of the River Jordan, and John baptized him. As Jesus came up from under the water, John saw a strange thing. What appeared to be a dove from heaven alighted on Jesus. Then John heard God saying, "This is my Son, whom I love. I am very pleased with him." Now the prophet knew that his cousin, Jesus, was the promised Lord.

Jesus in the Desert

After he was baptized, Jesus went into the desert to fast and pray to God about the work that lay ahead of him. God had given Jesus great power to heal the sick and perform miracles that would make people believe in him. But the Devil, the enemy of God, was determined to make Jesus disobey his Father, and to use his power in the wrong way.

Jesus was in the desert for a long time, and he felt extremely hungry. "If you are the Son of God," the Devil said to Jesus, "you could turn these stones into bread and eat them."

But Jesus refused to use his power to satisfy his own needs. "The Bible says that we cannot live by bread alone," answered Jesus, "but we must live by the words of God." Jesus knew that the most important thing was to obey God.

The Devil tried again to tempt Jesus. "If you threw yourself from the top of the temple in Jerusalem, the Bible says God would rescue you. Everyone would be astonished by your power."

But Jesus replied, "The Bible also tells us not to test God just for our own whims and desires." Jesus was not going to use God's power to make himself look clever.

For a third time, the Devil tried to make Jesus forget God's plans. "You could rule over the whole world," he said, "if you gave up God's will and followed me instead."

But Jesus had heard enough. "Get away from me, Satan!" he cried. "The Bible says that we must only worship and serve God."

So, the Devil left Jesus, and God sent his angels to strengthen him after his battle with evil.

When Jesus came out of the desert, he travelled to Galilee. John the Baptist had gone ahead of him, preparing the way. It was now time for Jesus to start his work, and he was looking for people who would help him.

As Jesus walked beside the Sea of Galilee, he saw some fishermen cast their nets into the lake. Their names were Andrew and Simon Peter. "Come, follow me!" said Jesus. "I will make you fish for men, instead!" So, straight away, Simon Peter and Andrew dropped their nets, and followed Jesus.

A little further on, Jesus saw some other fishermen cleaning and mending their nets. They were James and his brother, John. "Follow me!" called Jesus. Without a moment's hesitation, the two brothers left what they were doing to their father and his servants, and went with Jesus.

Later, Jesus gathered more followers until he had twelve in all. He called these men his disciples. Later, as more and more people followed Jesus, the twelve chosen followers were called 'apostles', or 'messengers', because they went out into the world and told others about the kingdom of God.

As well as James, John, Andrew and Simon Peter, there was Philip, Bartholomew, Thomas, Thaddeus, Simon (the patriot), James (son of Alphaeus), Matthew the tax-collector and Judas Iscariot.

The Wedding at Cana

Not long after Jesus had called his disciples to follow him, they were all invited to a wedding at Cana, in Galilee. Jesus' mother, Mary, was also one of the guests.

There were many people at the wedding feast, and the hosts gave them the best food and wine they could afford. The servants waited on the guests, offering them more of the sumptuous food and fine wine whenever they needed it.

But, behind the scenes, there was a terrible panic. One of the servants had realised the hosts had run out of wine. They did not know what to do. In those days, people could not just go to the shops and buy some more. It would bring disgrace and embarrassment on the family if they could not entertain their guests properly.

Jesus' mother overheard the murmurings in the background. She was a great friend of the family and wanted to help in some way. Mary whispered to Jesus, "They've run out of wine!"

Jesus realised that his mother was wanting him to use his power to save the day. But he also knew that he must now obey God and not his mother. "Why are you involving me in this problem?" he asked her. "I can only act when God tells me."

Mary listened to her son, but she still said to the household servants, "Do whatever my son tells you to do." She was sure that God would allow Jesus to help their friends.

Jesus looked around. Nearby, there were six enormous stone water jars. These had each contained twenty or thirty gallons of water at the beginning of the feast. Now they were empty as the guests had used the water for washing their hands before eating the meal. In those days, because of religious rules, the Jews washed their hands many times as part of a ceremony, so large amounts of water were necessary for a party such as this.

Jesus beckoned one of the servants. "Fill those jars with water again," he said. So, the servant did as he had instructed. "Now, pour some out and take it to the guests," said Jesus.

So, the servants took jugs of water and served it to the merrymakers. The first person to taste what they poured exclaimed to the bridegroom, "My goodness, what fine wine! Most people serve the best wine first and the cheapest last, but you have saved the best to the end!"

The guests had no idea where this wine had come from. But the servants and the disciples knew, and they marvelled at what had happened. This was the first miracle that Jesus performed. Because of it, the disciples realised that their leader was very special, and they put their faith in him.

Jesus heals the Sick

After the wedding at Cana, Jesus went with his disciples to Capernaum, where they stayed for a few days.

On the Sabbath day, Jesus went to the synagogue and, while he was there, he was invited to preach. The people listened and were amazed at Jesus' teaching. He spoke about God to them with great wisdom and power. No other priests or teachers had ever spoken like that before.

As Jesus preached to the Jews gathered there in the synagogue, he suddenly heard a terrible scream. A wild-looking man ran out of the crowds and shouted at him. "What do you want with us, Jesus of Nazareth? Have you come to destroy us?" The mad voice cried out, "I know who you are. You're the holy one from God!"

Jesus knew that the man was ranting and raving because his mind had been taken over by an evil spirit from the Devil. Just as he had tried to tempt Jesus in the wilderness, the Devil takes over people, to keep them from following God.

So, Jesus calmly, but sternly, spoke to the evil spirit. "Be quiet," he said. "Come out of that man!" The power of God is stronger than any force of the Devil, so the evil spirit had to obey. Immediately, the wild man shook violently and, with a shriek, the angry spirit left him. The man stopped shouting and became quiet and peaceful.

Those that saw this were stunned by what had happened. "Who is this preacher?" they asked each other. "He speaks with such knowledge and he has the power to make evil spirits obey!"

After Jesus had left the synagogue, he and the disciples went to the home of Peter and Andrew, which was in Capernaum. When he arrived, Jesus heard that Peter's mother-in-law was in bed with a terrible fever. "I'm very worried," said Peter's wife. "My mother is so frail, and she's desperately ill."

Jesus went to where the woman was lying. Very gently, he took her hand. As he touched her, the woman's fever left her and she felt much better. Jesus held her hand and helped the lady to get up. Soon the woman who had been feeling weak and ill was busying around her kitchen, cooking a meal.

When the neighbours saw Peter's mother-in-law hurrying about preparing food for her guests, they were amazed. They all knew how ill she had been. "Look, she's well again!" they whispered. "Jesus has healed her!"

That evening, a large crowd gathered outside Peter's house. Amongst them were many people suffering from all kinds of diseases. Some were crippled, lame, blind or deaf. Others had brought their relatives who were troubled by evil spirits.

Jesus came out to them. He touched and healed many people, and showed them all the greatness of God's power and love. Soon news of this had spread throughout the whole region of Galilee.

Jesus heals a Leper

After a few days, Jesus and his disciples left Capernaum, and went out into other areas of Galilee, preaching in the synagogues and healing the sick.

One of the worst diseases at that time was leprosy. It was an incurable illness and those that had it were considered unclean. No one would touch a leper, and those with the disease had to live separately from other people.

As Jesus travelled around the villages of Galilee, a man with leprosy came towards him. The poor, sick man fell on his knees in front of Jesus. "Lord," he said. "I know that if you want to, you can make me well again."

Jesus was filled with love and pity for the man who begged at his feet. He was lonely and ill, and no one would touch him for fear of catching the disease. "I want to make you well," said Jesus. And he reached out to the leper and touched his skin. "Now you are well!"

Immediately, the leprosy left the man and he was cured. The man was overjoyed, but Jesus said to him, "Don't tell this to anyone. Go and show yourself to the priest and offer sacrifices to God to thank him for your healing." But the cured man could not keep his joy a secret. Instead, he told everyone he met what Jesus had done for him. As a result, Jesus could not visit any town without attracting large crowds.

A few days after he had healed the leper, Jesus returned to the small fishing town of Capernaum. Many people came to hear him preach at the little house where he was staying. Those eager to hear Jesus filled the house, and even gathered outside the door. There was no room left for anyone else to come near.

As Jesus was teaching, four men arrived at the house. They were carrying between them a large mat, on which lay their sick friend. The man was paralysed, and could not move. People were jostling and pushing to hear Jesus speak, so, as the men approached, they realised it would be impossible to take their friend through the door.

"Sorry lads, there's no room to get him in there!" said one of the crowd outside.

"Everyone wants to see Jesus!" said another. "You'll have to wait your turn."

The four men had struggled a long way, carrying their friend. They were determined to get him to Jesus. They knew he would then be healed. Then one of them noticed the steps leading up to the flat roof of the house.

"I've had an idea!" he said. "Come on! Let's get him up there!"

The Paralysed Man

So, the men carefully carried the paralysed man up on to the top of the tiny house. Then, little by little, they dug a hole in the mud roof. When the hole was wide enough, the four men tied ropes to the wooden structure supporting their friend's mat and, very gently, lowered him into the crowds gathered below.

"Look at that!" gasped some of the people. When Jesus saw how much effort the four devoted friends had made to bring the sick man before him, he was moved by their faith. He looked at the man lying paralysed on the mat. Jesus knew that, apart from his illness, the sick man had other things that were troubling him, too. So, he said quietly to him, "Son, your sins are forgiven."

The religious leaders, who were among the crowd, looked horrified. "Who does this man think he is?" they thought. "Only God can forgive sins!"

Jesus knew what they were thinking. "Why are you worried about the words I've just spoken?" he asked. "You may not be able to see that I have the power to forgive sins, but you can see that I have the power to heal." Then Jesus turned to the sick man. "Get up!" he said. "Take your mat and go home."

The man, who had been unable to move for so long, leapt to his feet, picked up his mat and walked happily through the crowds. Everyone who saw this was astonished and praised God. They realised that if Jesus had the power to heal like this, perhaps he *could* forgive sins, too.

Jesus calms the Storm

Jesus continued to travel all around Galilee preaching, teaching and healing the sick. Wherever he went, crowds of people flocked to be near him. Jesus often grew very tired, and sometimes he needed to get away from everyone to be alone and pray to God.

One day, Jesus had been teaching and healing people by the side of the large lake, called the Sea of Galilee. As the sun went down and evening drew in, Jesus suddenly felt very weary.

"Let's get into the boat," he said to the disciples, "and go over to the other side of the lake."

So, Jesus and his disciples climbed into their small fishing boat and, leaving the crowds behind them, set sail across the water. Jesus lay in the stern of the boat, with his head on a cushion. The lapping of the waves and the gentle rocking movement of the boat was very soothing, and soon he had fallen fast asleep.

As Jesus lay sleeping, storm clouds gathered and the sky turned black. The gentle breeze turned into a fierce wind, and the calm surface of the lake became a raging sea.

Huge waves came crashing down, filling the little boat. The disciples frantically tried to bail the water out but, no matter how hard they tried, the boat began to sink. They knew they were in trouble.

"We're going to drown!" they wailed, and they called out to Jesus to help. Those that were close to him were amazed to find that, despite what was happening, Jesus was still asleep.

The disciples shook Jesus to wake him up, saying, "Lord, look, we're in a terrible storm. Don't you care if we all die?" Jesus opened his eyes. The wind was howling and great, heaving waves were towering above him. Jesus stood up in the boat and looked out at the vast walls of water looming overhead. He watched the sail being buffeted and torn by the fierce wind. Then, showing no signs of fear, Jesus spoke to the wind and the waves. He said simply, "Be still."

Just as suddenly as it had started, the wind died down. The surface of the water changed from a swirling mass of waves to a calm, glassy pool. Jesus turned to his disciples. "Why were you so afraid?" he said. "Do you still have no faith?"

The disciples did not answer him. They just stared in wonder and amazement. "Who is this man?" they asked each other. "Even the wind and the waves obey his command!"

Jesus raises the Dead

W hen Jesus reached the other side of the lake, a large crowd again gathered around. A man called Jairus joined the many people pushing to reach Jesus. Jairus was an important religious leader from the local synagogue, and everyone knew and respected him.

Jairus knelt on the ground at Jesus' feet. "My little daughter is dying," he said. "Please come and put your hands on her and heal her."

So, Jesus went off with Jairus to his home. The crowds followed him, jostling and pushing each other to get as close as they could to Jesus.

As he walked with Jairus, Jesus suddenly stopped. "Who touched my clothes?" he asked.

His disciples were puzzled by his question. "Lord, there are many people pushing to be close to you," they said. "Any one of them could have touched you." But Jesus had felt power go out of him. He knew that someone had touched him, wanting to be healed.

Among the crowd was a woman, trembling with fear. She knew it was her fault that Jesus had stopped. She had been ill for a long time, and spent all her money visiting many doctors, who had failed to find a cure. In desperation, she had reached out to touch Jesus' cloak.

"Lord, it was me," she said as she knelt at his feet. "I thought that if I could just touch your clothes, I would be healed."

Jesus was moved by the woman's faith. "Dear lady," he said to her. "Your trust in me has healed you. Go in peace. You will now be well."

Meanwhile, Jairus was waiting anxiously for Jesus to visit his daughter. But one of his servants arrived with terrible news. "Sir, I'm sorry, but your daughter is dead. There is no use in bothering the teacher any more."

When Jesus heard this he said, "Don't be afraid, Jairus. Just believe and trust in me."

He took the disciples Peter, James and John, and continued on to where Jairus lived. There he found people in mourning, weeping and wailing for the dead little girl. "Why are you crying?" he asked them. "The child is not dead. She is sleeping." But the mourners just laughed at him.

Jesus sent everyone away, other than the child's mother and father and the three disciples. They went into the child's room. Jesus took her gently by the hand and said, "Get up, little girl."

Immediately, the child stood up and walked around. Everyone was astonished at what they saw. "Give her something to eat," Jesus told her delighted parents. "I think your daughter is hungry!"

The Death of John the Baptist

The king who ruled over Galilee at this time was another man called Herod. (He was the son of the terrible Herod the Great who had massacred the babies in Bethlehem when Jesus was a child.) King Herod knew of John the Baptist, and had heard him preaching to the people to repent of their wicked ways. Herod admired John for his courage to say things that people did not want to hear.

The king, however, was not pleased when John chose to speak out about something that he himself had done wrong. "It is not lawful to divorce your wife to marry the wife of your brother," John told the king. Herod knew John was right, but he did not like to be told how to behave by one of his subjects. The king wanted to kill John, but he was afraid of the anger of the Jewish people, who believed John was a prophet of God.

Herod's new wife, Herodias, hated John because he spoke against her, so she thought up a plan to be rid of him. First of all, the queen nagged the king about the prophet so much that he agreed to put John the Baptist in prison.

While he was in the dark dungeon, John grew very depressed. He even began to doubt that Jesus was the Son of God. John sent his supporters to ask Jesus if he really was the promised Messiah.

So, Jesus sent messengers back to John, saying, "Tell John what you see and hear. The blind see again, the lame walk, those with leprosy are cured, the deaf hear, the dead are raised, and the good news is preached to the poor."

Jesus knew that when John heard about the acts of healing, he would be convinced that Jesus was the Messiah. Jesus told those around him that John the Baptist was the greatest prophet that had ever lived.

Some time later, Herodias decided on her second plan of action. The queen had a very beautiful daughter called Salome. Herodias knew that the king admired Salome, so she asked her daughter to dance before Herod at his birthday feast.

The day of the party came, and there was a great banquet. After the guests had eaten and drunk their fill, the entertainment began. Salome danced as she had never danced before, and the king was captivated by the young girl's performance. "That was wonderful," he said. "You must have a reward! You may have whatever you request!"

Salome knew what she must ask for. Her mother, Herodias, had told her already. The princess cried out, "Your majesty, I want the head of John the Baptist!" The king was horrified. He was afraid to kill a man of God, but he could not go back on his word. He had promised Salome in front of everyone present.

So, very reluctantly, King Herod ordered his soldiers to go to the prison and execute John. The head of the great prophet was brought on a plate and given to Salome. Immediately, the girl presented it to her wicked mother, Herodias.

John's friends wrapped up his body and took it away to give him a proper funeral. They sent messengers to Jesus to tell him the terrible news.

The Five Loaves and Two Fish

The apostles, the twelve disciples chosen by Jesus, had by now watched him heal many people and perform countless miracles, so their faith in God was very strong. Jesus decided it was time to send the apostles out to pray for people. So, he sent them out in pairs, and gave them authority to preach and heal the sick. The apostles came back, and reported to Jesus everything that they had done and taught. They were all very excited at what had been happening, and how people had been healed when they prayed for them.

As Jesus and the apostles were talking together, once again crowds gathered round, wanting to hear the preacher and be touched by him. Jesus was still feeling sad about the death of his cousin, John, and he wanted to be away from the people and quiet for a while. So, he said to the disciples, "Come, let's find a place where we can be together and get some rest."

Jesus and his twelve apostles climbed into their boat, and set sail across the Sea of Galilee to find somewhere peaceful. But some of the people spotted them leaving, and watched to see where their boat was heading. The crowds they had wanted to leave behind ran to the place where the boat was sailing, and were there to greet Jesus as he arrived.

When Jesus and his disciples landed, they did not find the peace they desired. Thousands of people were clamouring to see them. "Oh no!" said the disciples. "Lord, send them away. Can't we just rest for a while?"

But Jesus looked at the faces of the people eagerly awaiting him. "I can't leave them," he said kindly. "They are like sheep without a shepherd." So, tired as he was, Jesus sat down and began to teach and preach to the crowds.

Jesus spoke to the people who had flocked to listen until it grew late in the day. By now, everyone was feeling very hungry. The disciples said to Jesus, "Lord, it's very late and we're miles from anywhere. Send everyone away so that they can go to the local villages and buy themselves something to eat."

But Jesus answered, "You give them something to eat." The apostles were stunned by his words. "There are over five thousand people out there," said Philip. "It would take almost a year's earnings to pay for enough food to feed that lot! Do you want us to spend that much money on bread?"

Then Andrew, another of the disciples, said, "There's a young boy here who says we can share out his lunch. There are five barley loaves and two small fish, but that won't go very far among so many people."

Jesus said calmly, "Divide the people into groups of fifty and tell them to sit down." So, the disciples urged the crowds to make themselves comfortable on the grass.

The Feeding of the Five Thousand

Jesus took the loaves and the fish, and thanked God for providing them. After that, he divided the food amongst the hungry people. Then an extraordinary thing happened. The more Jesus shared out the bread and fish, the more bread and fish seemed to appear. All the thousands of people that were waiting to be fed had something to eat.

When everyone had eaten their fill, Jesus said
to the apostles, "Go and collect any food that's
left over. We mustn't waste anything." So, the
twelve apostles went to pick up the leftovers.
Between them, they filled twelve baskets with
the remains of the food.

The people were astonished by what had
happened. "This man, Jesus, is very special,"
they said. "He must be the chosen one of God
we've all been waiting for."

Jesus walks on Water

After Jesus and his disciples had fed the five thousand hungry people, Jesus told the twelve apostles to get into the boat and go on ahead of him to Bethsaida. He then sent the crowd on their way, and went up the mountainside to pray. Jesus needed time on his own to talk to God.

By the time evening came, the apostles had travelled out to the middle of the lake, and Jesus was alone on the land. He looked out to where the disciples were in their boat, and could see them struggling against the weather. The wind was blowing in the wrong direction, so the disciples had taken down the sail and were rowing the boat in order to go the way they wanted.

Jesus could imagine the apostles straining at the oars, and he decided to go and help them. He began to walk towards them across the top of the water.

By this time, it was the middle of the night, and the only light was that of the moon and the stars. When the apostles saw a shadowy figure moving across the water in the dark, they were terrified. "It's a ghost!" they shrieked.

"Don't be afraid!" Jesus called to them. "It's me. I'm coming to help you."

Peter called out, "Lord, if it's you, tell me to come out and join you."

"Come!" said Jesus. So, Peter got out of the boat, and walked across the top of the water towards Jesus. But, suddenly, he felt the wind blowing against him, and he was afraid. As soon as he began to worry about his own safety, Peter started to sink.

"Lord, save me!" he cried out. Immediately, Jesus reached out his hand and caught Peter. "Why did you doubt me, Peter?" he asked.

As soon as they both climbed into the boat, the wind died down. The apostles were amazed by everything they had seen. They gaped at Jesus, saying, "You really are the Son of God!"

Jesus heals the Deaf and Blind

One day, as Jesus was on his travels, some people brought to him a man who was deaf and could hardly speak. "Please Lord," they begged. "Will you lay hands on our friend and heal him?"

So, Jesus took the man to one side, away from the crowd. He signalled to the man what he was going to do. First, Jesus gently placed his fingers in the man's ears. Then he spat on his own finger and touched the man's tongue. In those days, people believed that spittle could heal. So, Jesus was conveying to the deaf man that he was going to make him better.

After that, Jesus looked up to heaven and prayed. With a deep sigh he said, "Ephphatha!" which means, "Be opened!" Immediately, the man was able to hear sounds all around him. He opened his mouth to grunt a few words and he found that he could speak, too. Everyone could understand exactly what he said.

Those that witnessed this were astounded. "Jesus has done everything!" they gasped. "He even makes the deaf hear and the dumb speak."

After this, Jesus and his disciples went again to Bethsaida. There, a blind man was led out to Jesus. He took the man away from the crowds to a quiet place outside the village. Again, Jesus used his own spit to show he was going to heal.

This time, Jesus spat on the man's eyes and then very carefully placed his hands on them. "Do you see anything?" Jesus asked him. The man stared around him. Instead of terrible darkness the man could see bright light, colours and shapes.

"I think I can see people," he said. "They look like trees moving around."

So, Jesus touched the man's eyes again. "Now everything is clear!" cried the man. "I can see perfectly!" He was overjoyed.

"Go home and see your family," said Jesus. "Don't go back to the village."

Jesus continued on his travels. He and the disciples spent some time preaching and healing in the city of Jericho. As they were leaving the city, Jesus heard a voice calling, "Jesus, son of David, have pity on me!" It was Bartimaeus, a poor, blind beggar who lived only on the money that other people put into his bowl. He had heard the crowds talking about Jesus and his power, and Bartimaeus longed to be healed. Some of the people told the beggar to be quiet, but this made him shout all the more.

"Son of David," he cried. "Have mercy on me!"

Jesus stopped. "Call him," he said.

So, some of them went over to Bartimaeus. "Come on, then! Up you get! Jesus is calling you to him."

The poor beggar threw his cloak to one side, jumped to his feet and was helped over to where Jesus was.

"What do you want me to do for you?" Jesus asked him.

The blind man replied, "Lord, I want to be able to see."

"You will see," said Jesus. "Your trust in me has healed you. Now go home."

Immediately, the beggar received his sight. But he did not go home.

Now that he could see, Bartimaeus wanted to follow Jesus.

The Sermon on the Mount

Some of the Jewish religious leaders were frightened of the power that Jesus had. They did not want to listen to the way he preached about God, and banned him from their synagogues.

So, Jesus taught the crowds of people who followed him out in the open countryside.

One day, when there was a particularly large gathering, Jesus and his disciples went up on to a mountainside and sat down. There he began to teach the disciples all about God, and how best to live their lives.

"The happiest people are those who realise just how much they need God, and ask him every day to help, strengthen and forgive them," said Jesus. "The Lord will bless those who are eager to do what is right and turn away from their evil ways."

Jesus went on, "God is pleased with people who try to be kind and loving. He hates to see fighting and quarrelling, and blesses those who try to make friends and keep peace in the world. One of the hardest things to do is to love and obey God when life is difficult and people bully and tease you for sticking to God's rules. But God knows those who are true to him, and he will reward them greatly in heaven."

Jesus told the people that they were to be like salt and light. In those days, everyone used salt to stop meat and fish from going bad. God wanted his people to live their lives in a good, clean, wholesome way to set an example and stop the world from going bad.

"You are the light of the world," said Jesus. "If someone has a lamp they do not hide it away, but they put it on a stand so that people can see its light in the darkness all around. In this way, you must shine like a light in the world and let everyone see your good deeds and the joy that you bring because you love God."

The crowds listened eagerly to everything Jesus said to them. No one had ever taught them about God in this way before. They knew the ten commandments, but Jesus was helping to explain the law more clearly.

"You know that God has forbidden anyone to murder," said Jesus, "but God also knows what you are thinking. If you have wicked and angry thoughts against someone, it's like committing murder, too." Jesus went on. "So, before you worship the Lord and pray, make sure that you have mended any quarrels or forgiven those that have hurt you. No matter how hard you may find it, God wants his people to be loving and kind, and not full of hatred and bitterness."

"Some of you may think that if someone hits you, it's all right to hit them back," said Jesus. "But I tell you, God wants you to accept what they do to you, no matter what it is. Don't strike back, but love your enemies and try to do good to those who hate you. Give to everyone who asks from you, and do not demand it back. Remember, treat everyone as you would like to be treated yourself."

Jesus teaches People how to live

The crowds listened eagerly to all that Jesus had to say. He spoke wisely and explained things well.

"Don't make judgements about each other and criticise each other's behaviour," said Jesus, "because people will have the same attitude to you as you have to them. Before you look for faults in other people, think first about your own faults and put those right."

"If you forgive people the wrong things they do, you too will be forgiven for your own mistakes. If you give generously to others, you will find things will be given to you."

Jesus told the people to look at the trees. "A good tree doesn't bear bad fruit, and a bad tree doesn't bear good fruit. Each tree is recognised by its own fruit. So it is with people. A good man brings good things out of the good stored up in his heart, and an evil man brings evil things out of his heart."

Jesus knew that most of the people around him were poor. They struggled to earn a living and make ends meet. Some of them were envious of those who were rich.

Jesus spoke to them about God's attitude to money. "Don't worry about how you are going to live, and think about what you are going to eat and drink, or what clothes you should wear. Isn't life more important than food, and the body more important than clothes?"

Jesus pointed up at the birds flying around them. "Look at the birds," he said. "They don't toil away, storing things up for the future, but God feeds them. Aren't you much more valuable to God than them?"

Then Jesus pointed at the flowers. "And why worry about what you're going to wear? Look at the lilies growing in the field. They don't think about how they're dressed. Yet the great King Solomon in all his best robes did not look as beautiful as one of those flowers!"

"Your heavenly father knows all your needs," said Jesus. "If you love and obey him and are kind to others, God will look after you and provide everything necessary for your life."

Jesus advised rich people not to buy all sorts of expensive and beautiful things that they did not need, but to give their spare money away to the poor. "Don't store up treasures on earth where they can be destroyed or stolen, but store up treasures in heaven. When you meet God, he will remember how you gave your money away to help others."

"None of you can serve two masters equally well," said Jesus. "You are bound to prefer one to the other. In the same way, you cannot love both God and money."

Jesus encouraged the people to ask God for what they needed, and to believe and trust in him. "You all know how to give good gifts to your own children. So, your heavenly Father knows how to give to you, his children."

The Lord's Prayer

Jesus went on to tell his followers how to pray to God. The people were used to seeing some of the religious leaders praying in public. They often made a great display about saying their prayers. But Jesus told the people that this was not the way God wanted them to behave.

"When you pray, go into your room," said Jesus. "Close the door, and pray to your Father in heaven. Then God will see that you have been secret about it, and he will reward you." Jesus went on, "Don't think it's important to say long prayers and babble away just for the sake of it. Pray simply and honestly like this:

> 'Our Father in heaven,
> hallowed be your name,
> your kingdom come,
> your will be done
> on earth as it is in heaven.
> Give us this day our daily bread.
> Forgive us our sins
> as we forgive those who sin against us.
> And lead us not into temptation
> but deliver us from evil.
> For yours is the kingdom,
> the power and the glory for ever,
> Amen.'

The first five lines of the prayer Jesus taught are about praising God and telling him that we want to do his will. Our praise to God's glory and importance should always come first in our prayers.

We then move on to ask God for the food we need to live, and ask him to forgive our wrongdoings. But we can only ask God for forgiveness if we ourselves are prepared to forgive those who have hurt or upset us.

Then Jesus tells us to ask God to keep temptation away, so that we do not disobey his laws and do bad things. At the end of the prayer, we tell God how much we trust him to have power over everything that happens to us.

Jesus told his disciples that God listens to the prayers of those who are humble and are truly sorry for anything they have done wrong. God is not pleased with people who think they are better than others.

Jesus and the Pharisees

Some of the Jewish religious leaders were called 'Pharisees', or 'separate ones'. They gave themselves this name because they kept apart from anyone who did not live according to their strict code of behaviour. The Pharisees were very careful to obey every single rule that had been added on to the laws given by God to Moses, long before. Some of the rules had been made up by religious men over the years, and were added to what God had commanded.

One of these rules was connected with what to do on the Sabbath day. God had told Moses, 'Remember to keep the Sabbath day holy.' The Lord did not want people to work or earn a living on the Sabbath. As far as the Pharisees were concerned, this meant that no one should do anything at all on the Sabbath day, except worship God.

Many of the religious leaders were worried about the power Jesus had over the ordinary people. Some of the Pharisees looked for ways to trick Jesus and prove he was breaking the law.

One Sabbath day, Jesus went into the synagogue to worship, and he saw a man there with a deformed hand. The Pharisees watched closely to see what Jesus would do. They wanted to catch him out, healing someone on God's holy day.

Jesus said to the man with the paralysed hand, "Stand up in front of everyone!" Jesus asked the people, "What is lawful on the Sabbath – to do good or to do evil, to save someone's life or to kill them?" Everyone remained silent. They were afraid of offending their religious leaders.

The harsh faces of the Pharisees stared at Jesus, looking for ways to trap him, and he was angry at their uncaring attitude. Jesus was not going to stop helping a sick person just because it was the Sabbath. He knew God loved that man enough to heal him on his holy day.

"Stretch out your hand," Jesus said to the man. So, the man opened out his deformed hand and it was completely healed. The Pharisees were furious. They went out and began to plot against Jesus even more.

Later, the Pharisees went to listen to Jesus preaching, to see if they could catch him out by what he said. One of them called out, "Teacher, we know you always speak God's truth, and pay no attention to what men say. Tell us now, is it right that we should pay taxes to Caesar?" Jesus knew they were trying to trap him. He would be breaking the Roman law if he said 'no', and he would be unpopular with the Jews if he answered 'yes'.

"Bring me a coin," he said. So they did. "Whose portrait is this?" he asked them. "And whose name is written here?"

"Caesar's," they replied.

"Then give to Caesar what belongs to him," said Jesus, "and give to God what is due to God." The Pharisees were amazed at his answer, and could not find any fault.

Jesus predicts his Death

Jesus continued to travel around, teaching all those who wanted to listen. One day, he and his disciples set out for the villages around Caesarea Philippi. As they walked along the road, Jesus talked with the apostles. "What do people say about me?" he asked them. "Who do they think I am?"

"Some people think you are John the Baptist come back to life," answered one of them.

"Others say that you are Elijah returned from the dead," another added.

"Then there are those who think you are a new prophet," said a third apostle.

Jesus thought about all this for a while. "Who do you think I am?" he asked.

Peter answered, "You are the Messiah, God's chosen King."

Jesus was glad that his apostles truly believed who he was, but he told them not to tell everyone that he was the Messiah. He knew that people would want to make him king, and expect him to lead soldiers in battle to free them from the Romans. God had not sent Jesus to give them that kind of freedom.

Jesus also knew that his disciples did not really understand exactly why God had sent him. They, too, wanted a saviour to lead the Jews against their oppressors. So, Jesus began to prepare them for what was going to happen to him in the weeks ahead.

"Soon, I am going to go through a very difficult time," he told the apostles. "As you know, many of the Pharisees and chief priests are against me. They are planning to have me arrested, and eventually to put me to death." Jesus went on, "I will be killed, but after three days I will come back to life again."

Peter was horrified. "What! Lord, you can't let this happen. You have the power to stop them. We don't want our Messiah to die!"

"Be quiet, Peter," Jesus said firmly. "Do not be like Satan and persuade me against God's will. What you are suggesting is not what God wants."

By this time, crowds of people had gathered around, waiting for Jesus to preach to them. The apostles were still listening as he said to them all, "Anyone who follows me will not find it easy. You must do as I do and forget about the things that you want in this world. By giving up riches, success and your own desires, you may think you are throwing your life away. But, let me tell you this, you will be gaining a different kind of life – one that is filled with God's love and peace. That life will last for ever."

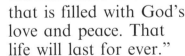

The Transfiguration

About a week later, Jesus took Peter, James and John with him, and went up the mountainside to pray quietly. Jesus needed to pray to his heavenly Father to strengthen him for the tough times ahead.

Jesus prayed for a long time, and his three followers sat a little way off, waiting for him. As time went by, and the day grew hotter, the apostles nodded off to sleep. But suddenly, something woke them up. Peter, James and John rubbed their eyes to make sure they were not dreaming.

There, in front of them was Jesus talking with two men, one on either side. But Jesus looked different. His face and clothes were gleaming with a dazzling brightness, like that of lightning when it flashes across the sky. A great radiance also shone from the two men, whom the apostles seemed to recognise as Moses and Elijah. They were talking about what was going to happen to Jesus soon in Jerusalem.

The apostles gazed in wonder at the three men bathed in such an unearthly light. Then Elijah and Moses began to fade away.

Peter was so overwhelmed by what he had seen he did not want it to end. He called out, "Master, this is a wonderful place! Let's put up three shelters here – one for you, one for Moses and one for Elijah!" He did not really know what he was saying.

As Peter was speaking, a great cloud enveloped the three apostles. God's voice spoke to them from the cloud, saying, "This is my son, whom I have chosen. Listen to him."

Then the cloud disappeared, and when the apostles looked towards Jesus, they saw that he was alone and seemed like his normal self.

Jesus joined them again, and they walked together back down the mountainside. The apostles were amazed and very moved by what had happened. But Jesus said to them, "Don't tell anyone what you have seen until I have risen from the dead."

Peter, James and John did not really understand what Jesus meant, but they knew that all they had experienced was very special and private and that, for now, they must keep it to themselves. They had just had a glimpse of God's great glory, which was something out of this world.

The Sower

When Jesus taught the ordinary people, he often told them stories about things that happened in everyday life. He did this to help explain about God's love and how he wants us to love him. These stories are called 'parables'. For those who want to understand Jesus' teaching, each parable has a meaning.

One day, when Jesus was teaching by the Sea of Galilee, there were so many people gathered along the shore, Jesus decided to climb into a boat and preach to the crowd from there. First of all, he told them the parable of the sower.

"Listen to this," he said. "There was once a farmer who went out to sow his seed in the fields. As he scattered the seed around him, some seed fell on the path. The birds saw it and quickly swooped down and ate it up."

"Other seed fell on rocky places where there wasn't much soil. It sprang up quickly, but couldn't put down deep roots because the soil was shallow. So, when the hot sun shone down on the little shoots, they withered and died."

"Some seed fell amongst thorns. When the plants grew up, the thorns choked them, so they couldn't bear fruit."

"Then there was the seed that fell on good soil. It took root, grew up strong and produced a good harvest."

When Jesus had finished the story, he said, "You have all got ears, now use them and listen well."

But the apostles who were close by were puzzled. "We don't understand what you're saying," they told Jesus.

Jesus said to them, "I use stories to explain about God, so that those who are really interested in the Lord will listen carefully, think about the story and understand it. Those who don't want to find out the truth won't bother to look for the meaning, and will be left in the dark." Then he explained the parable to the apostles.

"The farmer is the teacher, or person who spreads God's message. The seed is the word of God. Some people are like the seed sown along the path. As soon as they hear the word of God, the Devil comes along and makes them forget all about it."

"Other people are like the seed sown on rocky ground. They hear God's message and receive it happily, but as their belief is not deep-rooted, they soon give up on God when others tease or hurt them because of their faith."

"Then there are those like the seed that falls amongst thorns. They hear God's message, and want to live his way, but soon all their other desires and worries take over, and push God out of their thoughts."

"Finally," said Jesus, "there are those people who are like the seed sown on good soil. They hear God's message and take it into their hearts. Their belief is deep-rooted and strong, so they live a good life and show others that they are obeying God."

The Good Samaritan

One day, when Jesus was teaching, a well-educated religious leader stood up to ask him a question about God's laws. He wanted to test Jesus, to see how well he could answer.

"Teacher," he said to Jesus, "what must I do to gain eternal life?"

Jesus replied, "What is written in the law of Moses? You must know what it says."

The man answered, "It tells us to love the Lord God with all our hearts, souls, minds and strength. Also, it tells us to love our neighbours as we love ourselves."

"Yes, you're right," said Jesus. "If you do all that you will gain eternal life."

But the religious man continued, "What exactly does it mean by 'love your neighbour as yourself'? Who is my neighbour?"

Jesus told a story. "One day, a man was travelling from Jerusalem to Jericho when he was attacked by a gang of thieves. They beat the man up, robbed him, and left him half dead at the roadside."

"Not long afterwards, a priest came along the road and saw the man lying there, bleeding. 'That man looks dead to me,' he thought, 'and as a priest I am forbidden to touch a corpse. I had better not go near.' So, the priest went on his way and the man still lay there helpless."

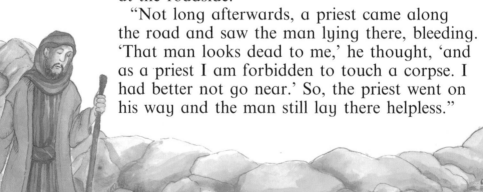

Jesus continued, "Then, a Levite, a religious man from the temple, came along the road. When he saw the man, he was frightened and crossed over to the other side of the road, and continued on his journey."

"At last, a Samaritan travelled the same route. As you know, the Jews and the Samaritans have always been enemies. But, this fellow stopped. He bent over the wounded man and saw that he was still alive. The Samaritan used his own wine and oil to clean and soothe the man's wounds. Then he tore his cloak to bandage the wounds and stop the bleeding."

"The good Samaritan heaved the weak man on to his donkey, took him to the nearest inn and looked after him all night."

"As he had to attend to business the next day, the Samaritan gave the innkeeper enough money to feed and care for the sick man. 'Look after him until I return,' he told the innkeeper. 'If this isn't enough money, I'll give you more later.' "

Jesus turned to the religious leader who had questioned him earlier. "So, which of these three travellers do you think was a 'neighbour' to the wounded man?"

The leader replied, "I suppose it was the one who was kind to him."

"Well," said Jesus, "go and be like him."

The Lost Sheep and the Lost Coin

When Jesus preached and healed the sick, he included everyone, whether they were considered 'good' or 'bad' people. Some of the most hated Jews at that time were the tax collectors, who gathered in the money to pay to the Emperor in Rome. Often, these tax collectors were dishonest, and kept some of the money they collected for themselves.

The Pharisees and other Jewish religious leaders were horrified that Jesus spent time with such people. "This man welcomes all the worst possible types," they muttered to each other. "He even eats with sinners!"

Jesus knew what the Pharisees were thinking, so he told the assembled crowd a parable. "Suppose one of you had a hundred sheep," he said, "but you lost one of them. What would you do?" He paused. "Would you forget about it and make do with the ones you had?" asked Jesus. "No, I think you'd want to find that precious sheep. Wouldn't you leave the other ninety-nine sheep safely grazing, and go out and search for the lost sheep until you found it? When at last, after a great deal of effort, you found your sheep, you'd be so pleased you'd carry it home, telling your friends and neighbours, 'Look! Isn't it marvellous? I've found the one that was lost!' "

The crowd nodded. Many of them were shepherds. They knew about looking after sheep, and how tiring it was to find those that went missing. "Well," said Jesus. "The way that you feel about finding your lost sheep is the way God feels about people who have gone the wrong way in life. He rejoices when someone who has sinned comes back to him and is sorry for their wrongdoings. In fact, there is more joy in heaven over that one lost person who is found than over ninety-nine good people who have always tried to obey God."

The Pharisees did not have time to respond before Jesus told them another little tale. "Then there's the story of the woman who had ten silver coins. One day, she found to her horror that she'd lost one. The woman quickly swept the floor, lit a lamp, and searched every nook and cranny until she found her missing money. When, hours later, she eventually did find the coin, she was so delighted she invited all the neighbours in for a drink to celebrate!"

Jesus explained, "In the same way that this woman and her neighbours were happy because of the lost coin that was found, so the angels of God are glad when a sinner returns to our heavenly Father."

The Lost Son

The Pharisees were still unmoved by Jesus' stories. They did not want to believe that God welcomes sinners who are sorry for what they have done. So, Jesus went on to tell a third story.

"Once there was a rich landowner who had two sons. The elder son was hard working and reliable, and helped his father run his farms. The younger son was not interested in staying at home. He wanted to go off into the world to travel and have a good time."

"The younger son knew that, one day, he would inherit half the estate, but he didn't want to wait that long. So, he went to his father and said, 'Father, can I have my share of the farms now?' His generous father agreed. He gave the lad a large amount of money and, not long afterwards, the younger son left home. He went away to a distant country and had a wild time spending all the money on women, drink and gambling."

"Soon, the young man had no money left. At the same time, there was a famine in that country. The younger son was desperate for somewhere to stay, so he tried to find a job. The only work he could get was feeding the pigs on a small farm. But even then, he still went hungry. The man who had once eaten nothing but the best food grew thinner and thinner until he became very weak. He was so ravenous, he was tempted to eat the dried-up scraps he was supposed to give to the pigs."

"Eventually, the younger son thought to himself, 'Even the men who work for my father have enough food to eat, and here I am starving to death! I will go home and throw myself on my father's mercy. I will tell him how sorry I am. He may not welcome me as his son, but he might give me a job on his farm.' So, the next day, he set off for home."

"While the young man was still some way from home, his father, who was out checking his flocks, caught sight of him. 'That thin, ragged fellow walks like my son!' he thought."

"As the man drew closer, the father saw that it was indeed his son, who had gone away. He was overjoyed to see the youth again, and took pity on his terrible state. The father ran to greet his son, flung his arms round him and kissed him."

Jesus went on, "The weary young man said, 'Father, I'm sorry, I've sinned against God and you. I'm not fit to be called your son.' "

"But the father ordered his servants, 'Quickly, bring the best robes you can find. Put sandals on his feet and my ring on his finger. Kill the calf we've been fattening up for a special occasion. We'll have a party and celebrate!' "

"So, that night, there was a great feast, with dancing and music and much good wine."

The Lost Son returns

Jesus continued the story. "Meanwhile, out in the fields, the elder brother had been working hard. He heard the music and laughter. 'What's going on?' he asked one of the servants."

" 'Your brother has come home,' replied the servant. 'Your father is having a party to celebrate that he's back, safe and sound.' "

"The elder brother was angry and refused to join in the feasting. 'I have worked hard for you all these years,' he said to his father. 'I've not disobeyed your orders or done anything wrong. You've never given me even the smallest party. Now look! The son who's thrown away all your money on having a good time comes back penniless and in rags, and you kill the prize cow in his honour!' "

" 'My son,' said the father, 'you are always with me and everything that I have is yours. But we have to celebrate and be happy. We thought this brother of yours was dead, and he's alive! He was lost, but now he's come safely home!' "

After he had told this parable, Jesus hoped that the Pharisees would accept and understand what he was teaching them. Like the generous and forgiving father in the story, God, our heavenly Father, forgives his children who are sorry that they have done wrong and return to him.

The Talents

Jesus warned his followers that he would not always be with them on earth. He told them that when they died, those who believed in him would go into God's kingdom. There, they would live for ever with Jesus.

Jesus wanted Christians to know that while they were still in the world, they should make the most of the abilities and opportunities that God had given them, to serve him in the best way possible. Then, when they eventually came before God, he would reward them according to how they had worked for him.

So, Jesus told them a parable to help explain this. "There was once a man, who had to go on a long journey," said Jesus. "He called his servants to him and instructed them to look after his property. Then he divided up his money between them, bearing in mind their abilities."

"To the first servant he gave five thousand gold coins, to the second he gave two thousand gold coins, and to the third he gave one thousand gold coins. Then he went on his journey, leaving them in charge."

"The first servant used his money to invest in shrewd business deals, and he made another five thousand gold coins to add to the first five. The second one also cleverly doubled what he had been given. But the third servant did nothing at all with his money. Instead he buried his gold coins in the ground!"

Jesus paused, then said, "After a long while, the master returned. He sent for the servants and asked for an account of the money he had entrusted to them."

"The first servant explained how he had managed to double the money he had been given. 'Well done!' said the master, 'You have been a loyal, trustworthy servant and used well what I have given you. Now I see how capable you are, I shall put you in charge of many things. Come and join my celebrations!' "

"Then the second servant also reported on how he had cleverly used his two thousand coins. 'Well done!' said the master. 'You, too, have been faithful and hardworking. You will be rewarded by promotion. Come and join the party!' "

"Finally, along came the third servant who had done nothing at all with what he'd been given. 'Master,' he said, 'I know you are a tough businessman. I was afraid to lose your money, so I buried it in the ground. Here it is, safe and sound.' "

" 'You worthless, lazy servant!' said the master. 'If you were so fearful, the least you could have done with my money was to put it on deposit in the bank. There it would have been safe and earned some interest, too!' "

"So, the master took the money from the lazy servant and gave it to the first servant who had worked so hard. 'Those who make full use of what they are given will be given more,' he said. 'People who cannot make use of what little they have, will lose that also.' "

" 'Throw this servant out,' the master said to the others. 'He has wasted his opportunity to do some good and has no place in the celebrations.' "

The Rich Fool and the Widow

One day, as Jesus was talking to the people, a man pushed his way to the front of the crowd. "Teacher," he said to Jesus. "My father has died, and my brother has taken over all his property. Tell him to divide the inheritance in two and give me my share."

Jesus answered, "I am not here as a judge to settle cases like that." Then, he turned to those gathered around him. "Watch out!" he said. "Don't become greedy. Life is not about how many possessions you own."

Then he told them a parable. "There was once a rich farmer whose land was very fertile. One particular year, he had such a good harvest he had no room to store all the crops he had grown. 'I know what I'll do,' he said to himself. 'I'll take down the barns I have now, and build much larger ones. Then I can store away all my grain and goods. I'll have so much saved up that I won't need to work for years. I'll take life easy and have a good time.' "

"But, that night, God spoke to the man. 'You fool!' he said. 'Tonight you are going to die. What will become of all your possessions now?' "

Jesus said, "That's what happens to people who collect riches for themselves here on earth, but do not store up treasures in heaven, by giving to others."

Jesus continued to teach the crowd about their attitude to money. Once, when he had been preaching outside the temple, Jesus sat down to rest for a while. He happened to be seated opposite the collection boxes, where people put money offerings to pay for the upkeep of the building.

Many rich people passed by and tossed large amounts of money into the boxes. Some made a great show of how many gold coins they were putting into the collection.

Then, a very poor widow came along and dropped into one of the boxes two very small copper coins. Jesus called his disciples over to him. "Did you see that woman put two small coins into the box?" he asked. "She has given more to the treasury than any of those rich people."

The disciples looked puzzled. "The rich gave only a small proportion of their great wealth," explained Jesus. "But that widow, in her poverty, gave everything," he said. "She put in all that she had to live on, and God knows that."

Jesus heals the Centurion's Servant

During his travels, Jesus again returned to the fishing town of Capernaum. Living there at the time was a Roman centurion. He was in charge of the eighty Roman soldiers who controlled that area of Galilee.

The Jews usually hated the Romans, but the people of Capernaum liked and respected this man as he was kind to them, and had even organised the building of their synagogue.

The centurion had a slave who was very ill. He was fond of his servant and did not want him to die. The Roman officer had heard all about Jesus healing the sick, so he asked the religious leaders of the synagogue to take him a message.

The Jewish elders approached Jesus and spoke about the centurion. "He's not like the other Roman soldiers," they told Jesus. "He admires and supports our nation so much he built us a place to worship."

So, Jesus went with the leaders to the centurion's home. He was not far from the house when the Roman officer came out to meet Jesus. "Lord, please don't trouble to travel all this way. I don't deserve someone as great as you in my home. That's why I didn't come and ask you in person."

The centurion went on, "Lord, I know that you only have to say the word and my servant will be healed. I am a man under the command of Rome, with many soldiers under my authority. I am used to giving orders. I only have to say, 'Go!' and a soldier does as I command. I say, 'Come!' and another soldier comes running. I know that if you order my servant to be healed, then he will be well again."

Jesus was astonished to find a Roman who had such trust in him. He turned to those around him. "I have not come across anyone, even out of all the Jews, who has shown so much faith as this man," he said.

Then Jesus said to the centurion, "Go home! Your servant is well again." The Roman officer returned to his house, and found that his slave had been healed exactly at the time Jesus had spoken.

Mary, Martha and Lazarus

Living in a place called Bethany, near Jerusalem, were two sisters called Mary and Martha, and their brother, Lazarus. They were all close friends of Jesus.

One day, Lazarus felt ill. Over the next few days he grew worse, and his sisters were very worried. "If only Jesus were here," said Mary, "he would make our brother better."

"We must send a message to him," said Martha. "I know he'll come. He loves Lazarus as much as we do."

Jesus was far away from Bethany. He had left that area as the Jews there had tried to stone him to death. So, it was some time before the news about Lazarus reached him. Jesus was upset when he heard his friend was ill, but he turned to the disciples and said, "This sickness will not end in death, but will bring glory to God." And, although he cared deeply for Lazarus, Jesus did not go to him straight away. Instead, he stayed in that place for another two days, preaching and healing the sick.

Then Jesus announced to the apostles that it was time to return to Bethany.

"Lord," they said, "remember what happened last time you were near there. It will be dangerous."

But Jesus was determined to visit Lazarus, and they set off at once.

On the journey, Jesus told the disciples, "Our friend Lazarus has fallen asleep, but I'm going there to wake him up."

"That's good," they replied. "If he's able to sleep, he'll soon get better."

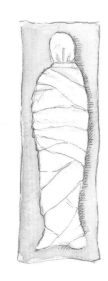

But Jesus went on, "I am trying to tell you that Lazarus is dead, but we will go to him. It's better that I wasn't there at the time, so that what you see will help you to believe in me."

The disciples were puzzled, but continued on with their master, looking out for any possible dangers that lay ahead.

When Jesus arrived at Bethany, Lazarus had been dead for four days. His body had been wrapped in cloth and placed in a tomb. Many Jews from Jerusalem had come to mourn Lazarus and were with Mary, weeping at the house.

Martha went out to meet Jesus when he was still far from their home. "Lord," she said. "If you had been here my brother would not have died. But I know that, even now, God will give you whatever you ask."

Jesus replied, "I am the resurrection and the life. He who believes in me will never die. Do you believe this?"

"Yes, Lord," Martha told him. "I believe that you are the Messiah, the Son of God." After saying this, she ran home to Mary to tell her that Jesus was on his way.

Immediately, Mary got up and went to find Jesus. The mourners followed her, thinking that she was going to the tomb. When Jesus saw Mary and the other Jews weeping, he felt very sad. "Mary, take me to where he is buried," said Jesus gently.

Then Jesus wept. Some of the Jews who were watching said, "See how he loved Lazarus!"

But others muttered to each other, "If this man can make the blind see again, why couldn't he stop his friend from dying?"

Lazarus is raised from the Dead

A large stone had been rolled across the entrance to the tomb where Lazarus lay, and Jesus asked them to remove it. "But Lord, there will be a bad odour," said Martha. "The body has been in there for four days."

"Did I not tell you that if you believed you would see the glory of God?" Jesus said.

Then Jesus looked up and prayed, "Father, thank you that you always hear my prayers. May everyone gathered here see that you give life to the dead, and will believe that you sent me."

After he had prayed, Jesus called out loudly, "Lazarus, come out!"

The crowd watched in astonishment as the dead man, still wrapped from head to toe in white linen, shuffled out of the tomb and stood before them all.

"Take off the grave clothes and free him," commanded Jesus.

Hurriedly, his sisters unravelled the strips of linen to reveal their healthy-looking brother.

"This man can raise the dead!" gasped some of the watching Jews. "He must be the Messiah!"

But others amongst them were terrified. They rushed back to Jerusalem, and told the Pharisees all they had seen and what Jesus had done.

"We must stop this man," the Pharisees said to each other. "If he carries on performing miracles such as this, everyone will follow him and we will lose our power."

From that day on, the chief priests and the Pharisees plotted to kill Jesus.

Jesus and the Little Children

O ne day, Jesus and his disciples were travelling to the fishing town of Capernaum. Jesus noticed that, on the journey, the apostles were deep in conversation about something. When they reached the house where they were staying, Jesus sat down ready to teach the waiting crowds. But before he began, he asked the twelve apostles, "What were you arguing about on the way here?"

His followers were embarrassed. They were ashamed because they had been discussing who, out of all of them, was the most important. "Who is the greatest in the kingdom of heaven?" the apostles asked Jesus.

He looked at the families who were gathering round to hear him speak. Jesus called a little child over to stand in the middle of them all. Then he said, "Let me tell you this. Unless you change and become like children, you will never enter the kingdom of heaven. Those who are ready to trust and obey me, like this child here, will be the greatest in God's kingdom."

Jesus went on, "Whenever someone welcomes and cares for a boy or girl like this for my sake, it's as if they are welcoming and accepting me. And whoever welcomes me, is welcoming God, my Father."

Another time, when Jesus was preaching in the region of Judea, many mothers brought their children to be touched by the Lord. It was the end of a long day, and the apostles could see that Jesus was very tired.

"Don't bother the Master," they said. "He's weary and needs some rest."

But Jesus was annoyed with his followers. "Don't send them away!" he said. "Let the little children come to me. My kingdom belongs to them, and to others who are just as humble, loving and full of trust."

So, the disciples called back the women with their toddlers and tiny babies. Very gently, Jesus took each of the little ones in his arms, put his hands on them and blessed them.

Mary anoints Jesus

Jesus had arrived in Bethany six days before the Passover. After he had raised Lazarus from the dead, a great dinner was given in Jesus' honour. Martha was serving at table, while Lazarus was among those eating with Jesus.

Meanwhile, their sister Mary had been thinking of a way she could show Jesus just how much he meant to her. The only thing of real value she possessed was a jar of very expensive perfume. Mary left the celebrations and went to fetch the jar.

When she returned, Mary knelt before Jesus and poured the exotic perfume over his bare feet. Then, with her long, dark hair she wiped his feet clean. The rich fragrance of the perfume filled the whole house.

Some of the men who watched this scoffed at such an act. Judas Iscariot, the disciple who later betrayed Jesus, said, "What a waste! The woman could have sold the perfume and given all the money to the poor. It was worth a year's wages." (Judas did not say this because he cared for the poor. He was in charge of the disciples' money bag and used to help himself to what was put into it.)

"Leave Mary alone," said Jesus. "She has done a beautiful thing for me as the time of my death draws near. The poor will always be among you, but you will not always have me. In the future, whenever people tell others about my life, they will also tell of Mary and what she did for me today."

Palm Sunday

Bethany, where Jesus was staying, was not far from the city of Jerusalem. Hundreds of people had travelled from all over the country to visit the temple for the Passover festival. News of Jesus and the astonishing miracle of Lazarus had reached the ears of many of these Jews, and they were eager to see Jesus for themselves.

Meanwhile, Jesus was also planning to head for Jerusalem. He said to the disciples, "Go to the village, and just as you enter it you will find a young donkey tied there. No one has ever ridden it before." Jesus continued, "Untie the donkey and bring it here. If anyone asks you what you are doing, tell them that the Lord needs the colt and will send it back soon."

So, the disciples went and found the donkey just as Jesus had said. When the people were told it was for Jesus, they were happy to let it go.

Jesus' followers brought the donkey to him, and threw their cloaks across its back. Although no one had ever ridden it before, the young animal was quite content to let Jesus sit on it. So, Jesus and his disciples set off for Jerusalem. The donkey stepped steadily up the steep road to the city, proudly carrying its precious load.

As Jesus drew near to Jerusalem, the crowds cheered. Some people spread their cloaks on the road in front of him, while others threw down palm branches to pave his way. Everyone waved to Jesus and welcomed him.

"Hosannah!" they cried. "Blessed is the one who comes in God's name! He is the king we have all been waiting for!"

When the Pharisees saw and heard these things, they were even more worried. "Look how everyone adores him!" they muttered to each other. "Somehow, we have to be rid of this man, Jesus."

Jesus in the Temple

When Jesus arrived at Jerusalem he went straight to the temple to observe everything that was happening in the courtyard there. But, because it was late in the afternoon, he did not stay long and, with the twelve apostles, returned to Bethany where they spent the night.

The next morning, Jesus and his disciples set off once again for Jerusalem. His followers noticed that Jesus was angry and upset about something and, once they arrived at the temple, they found out why.

In the courtyard of the temple, traders had set up market stalls to sell their goods to the pilgrims flooding in to celebrate the Passover. The visitors wanted to buy animals or birds to sacrifice to God, and the unscrupulous salesmen were charging high prices and taking advantage of the poor.

Tax-collectors and money-changers also cheated the Jews who had travelled from far away to worship at God's holy place. Other traders were using the courtyard as a shortcut through the city streets, and were carrying all kinds of merchandise back and forth.

Jesus could not believe his eyes. He was horrified. This was his Father's house, a holy place, built especially for prayer and worship. Yet the temple priests allowed all this shady business to be done within its walls.

In a fit of rage, Jesus lashed out at the traders and knocked over their stalls. "God said that his house was to be a house of prayer, where people from every nation could come to worship him!" cried Jesus. "But you have turned it into a den of thieves!" And he drove out the money-lenders and hurled their coins to the floor.

The people were amazed at Jesus' courage. He was not afraid to speak the truth and stand up to the priests and the wily tradesmen. The Jewish people understood what he was saying, and listened well to his teaching.

But, when the chief priests and teachers of the temple heard about this outburst, they were more determined than ever to kill Jesus.

The Plot against Jesus

From then on, the Pharisees and chief priests watched for any possible way to trick Jesus. They wanted to arrest him, but knew they would have to have a good reason to do so in front of the people.

Jesus knew what they were plotting and, one day, as he was teaching in the temple, he told a parable which the Pharisees could plainly hear.

"There was once a man who planted a vineyard," Jesus told those around him. "He put into it everything that was necessary to make good wine. Then he rented the vineyard to some tenant farmers and went on a journey."

"At harvest-time, the man sent a servant to the tenants in order to collect some of the fruit from the vineyard. But the farmers seized the servant, beat him up and sent him away empty-handed. Then he sent another servant, and he too was treated badly. So, the owner sent a third servant, and this one they killed. Over a period of time, the man sent more servants and, like the others, they were either beaten up or murdered."

Jesus continued, "Finally, the owner of the vineyard decided to send his son, whom he loved dearly. 'They will treat my own son well,' he thought. 'They will respect *him*.'"

"But, when the tenants saw the son, they plotted amongst themselves, saying, 'This is the son and heir. If we kill him, we'll inherit the vineyard ourselves!'"

Jesus went on, "So, the tenant farmers took the man's precious son, killed him and threw him out of the vineyard."

"What do you think the owner of the vineyard will do now?" asked Jesus. He paused, then he told them, "The owner will come and kill those tenants and give the vineyard to others."

Those that were listening knew that 'the vineyard' was the Jewish nation, and that 'the owner' was God. The chief priests had been put in charge by God. Over the years, the Lord had sent many prophets, who had been killed or ignored. Now he had sent his son, and 'the tenants' were planning to kill him, too.

When they heard the parable, the Pharisees were furious. So, they held a meeting at the palace of the high priest, Caiaphas. "We have to think of a way to arrest this troublemaker," they said. "But we can't do it during the Passover, or there'll be a riot."

While the Pharisees and chief priests were plotting Jesus' death, one of his disciples, Judas Iscariot, paid them a visit. Judas had decided not to stay with Jesus any more. He wanted power and riches, not a life of serving others and helping the poor. He had expected the Messiah to be a mighty warrior king, and had hoped to be one of his twelve chosen ministers.

"How much will you give me if I tell you where and when you can arrest Jesus?" Judas asked the priests.

The Pharisees could not believe their luck. Jesus had been betrayed by one of his own disciples!

"We'll give you thirty silver coins," they said. And they counted out the money straight away. So, Judas took the silver and, from then on, he looked for a way to hand over his master.

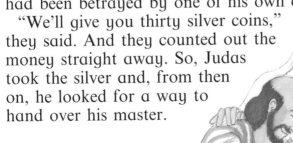

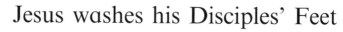

Jesus washes his Disciples' Feet

At the Feast of the Passover, the Jews eat a special meal of lamb with bitter herbs and bread with no yeast. At this time, they remember how God freed his people from slavery in Egypt, and how the Angel of Death 'passed over' their homes.

"Where do you want us to prepare the Passover meal?" the disciples asked Jesus.

He gave them instructions about how to find a suitable place. "Go into the city," he said, "and a man carrying a water jar will meet you. Follow him, and he will take you to a house. When you get there, ask the owner to show you where we are to eat the Passover supper. He will take you to a large room upstairs. It will be furnished already, and you can make all the preparations there."

So, the disciples did as Jesus commanded. They found everything just as he had said and prepared the celebration meal.

That evening, Jesus and the twelve apostles gathered in the room to eat their last supper together. Jesus knew that the time had come for him to leave this world and go to his Father in heaven. He was also aware that Judas was looking for a way to betray him, and accepted that this was all part of what was planned.

Before he went, Jesus wanted to show his disciples how much he loved them. They were looking forward to eating together, but had arrived hot and dusty from their walk.

As the food was being served, Jesus took a bowl of water and a towel. Then he knelt down and began to wash his disciples' feet.

In those days, to wash the feet of others was the job of the lowliest servant. The disciples were amazed and very moved that their master should do this for them. But when it was the turn of Simon Peter, he could not bear it. "Lord, I can't let you wash my feet!" he exclaimed.

Jesus replied, "Unless I wash you, Peter, you have no place with me."

Peter wanted to show Jesus how much he loved him. He said, "Then Lord, in that case, don't just wash my feet, but wash my hands and face, too!"

"Those that are clean need only to wash their feet," Jesus answered. "You are clean," Jesus told Peter, "but not every one of you is." (Jesus was referring to Judas, and showing them that he knew there was one of them who was not loyal and honest.)

When he had finished washing their feet, Jesus returned to his place at the table. "Do you understand what I have been trying to show you?" he asked his disciples. "You call me your Lord and master, and that is what I am. Yet, as your Lord, I am willing to do anything for you because I love you. I want you to follow my example. Remember, no person is more important than another. Love one another as I have loved you."

The Last Supper

As Jesus and his disciples were eating their last meal together, Jesus said, "I tell you the truth, one of you is going to betray me."

The disciples were horrified. "Lord, who is it?" some of them asked. "Is it me?"

"It is one of the twelve," answered Jesus. "One who is eating here with me now. But the man who betrays the Son of God will wish he had never been born!"

Then, during the Passover meal, Jesus did something special so that, in the future, his Christian followers could always remember him. He took the loaf of bread, gave thanks to God for it, and divided it into pieces. Jesus gave the bread to his disciples, saying, "Eat this, all of you. This is my body, which I am going to give up for you. Do this to remember me."

After that, he took the large cup of wine. Again, he thanked God for it and offered it to his disciples, saying, "Drink from this, all of you. This is my blood, which is going to be shed for many. My blood will be the seal of a new promise which God will make with all people, that he will forgive their sins." The disciples were puzzled, but did as Jesus told them.

As they ate the food, Jesus dipped some bread in the herb sauce and handed it to Judas. "Be quick about what you are about to do," he said. The other apostles did not understand why Jesus had said this. They thought that as Judas was in charge of the money, Jesus had instructed him to go and pay for something. As soon as Judas took the bread from Jesus, he went out.

Then Jesus talked more with his apostles. "I will not be with you much longer. Where I am going you cannot follow now but you will later."

Simon Peter was very upset at the thought of losing his master. "Lord, why can't I follow you now?" asked Peter. "I would die for you."

Jesus answered, "Peter, I tell you the truth that before the cock crows to announce tomorrow's dawn, you will disown me three times."

"Even if I have to die with you, I will never disown you!" said Peter. All the others agreed.

"I am going to my Father to prepare a place for you," said Jesus. "One day, I will come back and take you to be with me. You know where that place is."

But Thomas was puzzled. "Lord, we don't know where you are going," he said, "so how can we know the way?"

"I am the way to God," said Jesus. "No one can reach the Father unless they believe in me."

Then Jesus told his apostles that they would not feel alone when he had gone as God would send his Holy Spirit to guide and help them.

"Before I leave you, I want to give you my peace. This is something that you cannot find in this world. Do not be worried or afraid. If you trust in me, you will be given new strength and joy, no matter how hard your life may be."

Jesus prepares to die

Then Jesus went out with the disciples to the Mount of Olives. In a place called Gethsemane, there was a peaceful garden where he often liked to pray.

Judas Iscariot knew that, after supper, Jesus would go there with his disciples. Judas had decided that the Garden of Gethsamene would be the ideal place to have Jesus arrested. There would be no crowds of supporters and so no danger of a riot.

When Jesus arrived at Gethsemane, he was feeling very troubled. "Sit here while I go over there to pray," he told the disciples.

Then, taking Peter, James and John with him, he went to a secluded part of the garden. "Please, stay with me and keep watch," he said to the three apostles. "My heart is heavy and I feel I could die of sorrow."

Then, just a short distance away from them, Jesus fell on the ground and prayed to God. "My Father," he said, "if possible, don't let me go through the terrible suffering that lies ahead. You can do anything; you are able to save me from this. But, if you want it to happen, let me do what pleases you, not what is easier for me." Jesus was so anxious that, as he prayed, the sweat poured from him like great drops of blood.

When he turned to his three friends, Jesus found they had fallen asleep. "Could you not just stay awake with me for one hour?" he asked Peter, sadly. "Get up and pray, so that you are not tempted to rest. You mean well, but your bodies are weak."

Then, twice more, Jesus went away to pray. Again he asked his heavenly Father to spare him the painful death which he would have to endure. God heard the prayers of his son, and he sent an angel to strengthen him for what he had to face.

When Jesus returned to his followers the third time, he said, "Are you still sleeping? You must wake up now. The time has come for the Son of God to be handed over to his enemies. Look, here comes the one who has betrayed me!"

Jesus is arrested

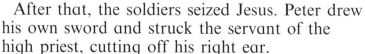

The disciples peered out sleepily into the night. They could see many shadows in the dark, and hear the sound of feet marching into the garden. Then they saw the glint of steel in the moonlight, and knew that there were people carrying swords. The apostles leapt to their feet.

Then the disciples caught sight of Judas. He was leading a crowd of soldiers and officials towards them. Judas was muttering to the guards, "The one I kiss is the man to arrest."

As he approached Jesus, Judas leant forward to kiss him. "Good evening, Master," he said.

Jesus replied, "Judas, are you going to betray the Son of God with a kiss?"

After that, the soldiers seized Jesus. Peter drew his own sword and struck the servant of the high priest, cutting off his right ear.

"Put your sword away, Peter," said Jesus. "Those that live by fighting will die that way. If I called out to my Father, he would send twelve legions of angels to protect me. But I must do what God has planned."

Then Jesus touched the ear of the wounded man and immediately it was healed.

Jesus turned to the chief priests and officers of the temple guard, who had come for him. "Am I supposed to be leading a rebellion? Why have you come with weapons against me?" he asked. "Every day, I was with you in the temple court, and you didn't lay a hand on me. But you choose to do your evil business in the dark!"

Jesus continued, "Carry on, this must all take place, so that what was foretold by the prophets should happen."

When the disciples saw that Jesus had been arrested, they deserted him and fled.

Peter disowns Jesus

Peter watched to see where the crowd took his master, and followed at a safe distance. They marched Jesus to the house of Caiaphas, the high priest. There, he was put on trial before the chief priests and the Pharisees.

Peter went as far as the courtyard of the house and waited around nervously, mingling with the guards that were gathered there. As he sat with the soldiers, warming himself by the fire, a servant girl came up to him. "Weren't you a friend of that Jesus of Nazareth?" she asked, peering at him closely in the firelight.

Peter panicked. "No," he answered. "I don't know the man!"

He moved away from the fire, and wandered over to a gateway nearby.

Another servant noticed him, and called out, "This fellow over here is one of that lot from Galilee!"

Again, Peter denied that he knew Jesus. "I'm nothing to do with him," he said.

Some time later, as Peter was talking with with one of the crowd, a man came up to him and said, "Here, you! You're one of that man's followers, aren't you? You've got an accent like his! And I saw you in that olive grove near Gethsemane!"

"I don't know what you're talking about!" Peter answered.

As soon as he had spoken, Peter heard a cock crowing, and the cold light of dawn lit up the sky. Then Peter remembered what Jesus had said: "Before the cock crows to announce the dawn you will disown me three times."

Peter looked up. In the distance, he could see the face of Jesus, his Lord and master, staring out from the trial he endured. Their eyes met, and Peter felt desperately ashamed.

He loved Jesus so much, yet he had just been cowardly, weak and disloyal. Peter left the courtyard and wept bitterly.

Jesus on Trial

I nside the house, the high priest questioned Jesus about his disciples and his teaching. The Jewish leaders had tried to find false evidence against Jesus, but none could be found.

Eventually, Caiaphas asked him, "Are you the Christ, the Son of God?"

"I am," answered Jesus.

At this reply, the high priest tore his clothes in rage. "We don't need any more evidence," he cried. "This man is guilty of blasphemy!"

And he turned to the others assembled there. "What do you think?" he asked. "He claims to be the Messiah!"

They all agreed that Jesus should be sentenced to death. Some of them spat on him. Then they blindfolded him, and hit him with their fists. The guards took Jesus away and beat him, too.

As the Jews were ruled by the Romans, Jesus had to be tried by Roman law before he could be executed. So, early in the morning, the Jewish leaders bound Jesus, and led him away to the palace of the Roman governor, Pontius Pilate.

When Judas saw that Jesus was condemned to death, he suddenly felt terrible remorse. He took the thirty silver coins back to the Pharisees. "I have done wrong," he said. "I have betrayed an innocent man!"

"That's not our problem," they answered him, "it's yours." Judas hurled the money into the temple. Then, unable to stand the guilt, he went away and hanged himself.

Meanwhile, Jesus stood before Pilate.

"He's a troublemaker," the Pharisees told the governor, "and he claims to be a king." The Jewish leaders accused Jesus of many false things, to which he made no reply.

Pilate questioned Jesus for a long time, and found him guilty of nothing. "I find no reason to execute this man," he told the Jewish leaders.

At the time of the Passover, there was a custom that one prisoner could be released on request. In the dungeons at that time was a man called Barabbas. He was accused of rioting and murder. To keep the crowds happy, Pilate offered to release a prisoner to them.

"Shall I release the King of the Jews?" he asked them.

But the chief priests and the Pharisees had urged the mob outside to shout against Jesus. "We want Barabbas!" they cried out. "We want Barabbas!"

"Then what shall I do with the one you call the king of the Jews?" asked Pilate.

"Crucify him!" they shouted. "Crucify him!"

Pilate was very wary of executing an innocent man. "Why?" he asked them. "What crime has he committed?"

But the people just shouted even louder, "Crucify him!"

The Roman governor was not happy. He took a bowl of water and, in front of the crowd, he washed his hands. "I am innocent of this man's blood," he said. But he had Jesus flogged, and handed him over to be crucified.

Golgotha

After Jesus had been brutally whipped, the guards took him into the courtyard of the palace. "So, you think you're a king, do you?" they said. "We'll see about that!"

The soldiers stripped Jesus, and dressed him in a purple robe. On his head, they placed a crown that they had made out of twisted thorns. Then the guards put a staff in his hand, knelt in front of him and mocked him.

"We salute you, King of the Jews!" they called out. Then they spat on Jesus, and used the staff to beat him on the head over and over again.

Once they had used him for their own amusement, the soldiers led Jesus off to be crucified. Usually, those who were to be executed each had to drag their own wooden cross outside the city to a hill, called Golgotha (the place of the Skull).

Jesus was so weak from the cruel flogging and beating, he was unable to carry his cross. The guards spotted a sturdy-looking African man, called Simon, coming towards them.

"You look fit enough," they said. "You can carry this man's cross to the place of execution."

When they reached the top of the hill, the soldiers made Jesus lie down on the large cross while they hammered long, sharp nails through his hands and feet to attach him to the wood. Then, they lifted up the cross and fixed it into the ground so that it stood upright.

There Jesus hung, his arms outstretched, dying an agonising death in the terrible heat. Above his head, the Romans had written, "This is Jesus, the King of the Jews".

The Crucifixion

The guards sat at the foot of the cross and decided what to do with Jesus' robe. "This is a good piece of cloth," one said. "Let's not tear it." So, they drew lots to choose which one of them would have the robe.

Then, the Pharisees and other Jewish leaders crowded round. They sneered and called out, "He saved others, let him save himself. He said he was the Son of God. Let God rescue him now!"

Others shouted, "If he is the Messiah, let him get down from the cross!"

Jesus looked at the faces of the Jewish leaders, filled with hate, and at the soldiers laughing below him.

He prayed to God. "Father, forgive them," he said, "for they don't know what they are doing."

On either side of Jesus, two robbers were also being crucified. One of them said, "If you are the Christ, why don't you save us all?"

But the other robber called out, "Shut up! We deserve our punishment, but this man has done nothing wrong." Then he turned to Jesus and said, "Lord, remember me when you come into your kingdom."

Jesus was filled with compassion for the thief who had repented. He answered him, "I tell you the truth, today you will be with me in paradise."

Near to the cross were many of the women who loved Jesus. When Jesus saw Mary, his mother, weeping, and the disciple, John, close by, he said to his mother, "Dear woman, this man will be your son from now on." And to John he said, "Look after her as if she were your own mother."

At noon, the sun was hidden, and darkness came over all the land. During the next three hours, Jesus grew weaker and weaker until the time came when he knew he was going to die.

"I'm thirsty," he whispered. And the guards soaked a sponge in wine vinegar and put it to his lips.

Finally, at three o'clock, Jesus cried out loudly, "It is finished! Father, I give my spirit to you."

Then he bowed his head, and died.

At the moment Jesus gave up his life, the great curtain of the temple was torn in two from top to bottom, and there was a huge earth tremor. When those that were guarding Jesus felt the ground shaking beneath them, and saw the dark sky above, they were terrified and cried out, "Surely this man was the Son of God!"

Jesus is buried

Jesus was crucified on a Friday, the day before the Jewish Sabbath. The Jews did not want dead bodies on show during this special day, so they asked Pilate if they could be removed.

A member of the Jewish Council, a rich man, called Joseph of Arimathea, was secretly a disciple of Jesus. He was a good, kind, honest man, who had not consented to the death of Jesus at his trial. He asked the Roman governor if he could give Jesus a proper Jewish burial. Pilate agreed to his request, and gave Joseph permission to take away the body of Jesus.

So, with a friend, called Nicodemus, Joseph carefully cleaned and bathed Jesus' body. Then, in accordance with Jewish custom, they wrapped it in strips of linen, and put the burial cloth round his head.

At the place where Jesus was crucified there was a garden, and in this place there was an empty tomb which had never been used. As it was almost time for the Sabbath, the two men took Jesus' body and laid it inside the tomb. They heaved and pushed a huge round stone across the entrance and went away.

Close by, the women who had cared for Jesus watched all that happened. Amongst them was Mary Magdalene. She saw where Jesus was buried. Then, as evening drew in, she sadly left the garden to respect the Sabbath day.

The Pharisees and chief priests were not content. Although they had successfully organised the execution of their enemy, they were still fearful. Once again, the Jewish leaders went to visit Pontius Pilate.

"Sir," they said, "we remember that while he was alive, this imposter, Jesus, stated that after three days he would rise from the dead."

The Roman Governor listened curiously. They continued, "So, give orders that the tomb where he is buried should be under guard until the third day is over. Otherwise, his disciples may come and steal the body and tell people that Jesus has been raised from the dead. If this were to happen, it would be an even worse crime than saying he was the Messiah!"

Pilate thought for a moment. Then he gave his orders. "Take a guard," he said. "and make the tomb as secure as possible."

So, the Jewish leaders hurried away. They put a seal on the stone across the entrance to the tomb, and placed Roman soldiers in front of it.

Jesus rises from the Dead

The next morning, at dawn, the women who mourned Jesus made their way to the tomb. They were carrying sweet-smelling spices which they would use to embalm his body.

"How are we going to get inside?" asked one, as they walked along. "We aren't strong enough to move that huge stone!"

As they drew near, however, the women saw that the stone had been rolled away from the entrance to the tomb, and the guards had disappeared. The women peered into the darkness to look for Jesus' body. But all that remained were the strips of linen, neatly folded where the corpse had been.

"He's gone!" cried one of them. "Someone must have stolen his body."

Suddenly, an angel appeared before them, and a dazzling light filled the tomb. "Don't be afraid," he said. "I know you are looking for Jesus, who was crucified. He is not here. Look, there is the place where they laid him. He has risen from the dead, just as he said he would. Go quickly and tell his disciples. He is going ahead of you into Galilee. There you will see him."

Trembling with fear and excitement, the women went out and fled from the tomb. Filled with joy, they ran to tell his disciples the good news.

When the women blurted out what they had seen and heard, the disciples did not believe them. So, Peter and John decided to go and see for themselves.

As soon as they arrived, Peter went straight into the tomb. It was all just as the women had described. The burial cloth which had been round Jesus' head was folded and lay separately from the other linen on the rock shelf. Then John looked in and he, too, could see that the body had gone.

The two disciples did not know what to think, so they left the garden and went home. But Mary Magdalene, who had been with them, remained behind. She stood staring unhappily at the empty tomb, and then began to cry.

As she wept, Mary heard a man's voice behind her. "Woman," he said, "why are you crying? Who is it you are looking for?"

Thinking it was the gardener, Mary asked, "Sir, if you have moved him, tell me where you have put my Lord."

Then, very gently, Jesus said, "Mary." As he spoke her name, the voice was unmistakable. It was the one she knew and loved so well. Mary quickly turned round and saw that it was Jesus.

"Master!" she cried out in joy.

"Go and tell my disciples that I have risen," said Jesus. "Say that I am going to return to my Father and your Father, to my God and your God. But, before that, I will appear to them in Galilee."

So, on that glorious Sunday morning, Mary Magdalene hurried back to the eleven disciples.

"I have seen the Lord!" she cried, her heart bursting with excitement. "He is alive!"

Jesus appears to his Disciples

On that same Sunday, two friends of Jesus were travelling to a village, called Emmaus, which was seven miles from Jerusalem. While they were walking along the road, they chatted about all the things that had been happening.

As the couple talked things over with each other, a stranger came up and walked along with them. "May I join you?" he asked. "You look upset. What's the matter?"

Cleopas and his friend stopped, and looked at the stranger sadly. "You must be a visitor to Jerusalem," said Cleopas, "if you don't know about what's been going on there recently!"

"What has been happening?" asked the stranger.

So, Cleopas told the man who had joined them all about Jesus of Nazareth, and how the chief priests and the Pharisees had plotted against him.

"They crucified him!" said Cleopas. "And we had hoped that he was the Messiah, the one who was going to save us all. Then, this morning, three days after his death, some women went to the tomb and found his body had gone. An angel of God appeared to them and said that Jesus is alive! We don't know what to make of it all."

The stranger listened carefully to what was said. Then he said, "But think about what the prophets of God predicted. It is written in the Scriptures that the Messiah had to die for the sins of other people, in order to bring them peace and forgiveness."

Then, as they travelled, the man explained the Scriptures in detail, and reminded them of how it was God's plan that the Messiah should rise from the dead because he had to overcome all evil.

When they arrived home, Cleopas invited their new friend to join them for supper. He was so wise and comforting, they wanted to hear more.

As they sat down to supper, the stranger took the bread, thanked God for it and handed it to them. It was then that they realised who was with them.

Cleopas and his friend suddenly saw that they had been walking and talking with Jesus. But, as soon as they recognised him, Jesus disappeared from their sight. "No wonder he could talk so well about God and the prophets!" said Cleopas. "Only Jesus can teach like that."

The couple were overjoyed. Immediately, they hurried out of the house, and ran to where the disciples were gathered together.

But, as they burst in through the door to tell everyone their news, they were greeted with the same message. "It's true!" cried the disciples. "We know the Lord has risen."

As they were chatting excitedly together, Jesus suddenly appeared in the room.

"Peace be with you," he said. They all stared in amazement. Jesus showed them his hands and feet, and they saw the marks where the nails had pierced him. Then, Jesus shared their meal and, once more, their master explained to them what God had planned.

The Miraculous Catch of Fish

One of the apostles, Thomas, was not there when Jesus appeared to the others. So, the other disciples told him, "We have seen the Lord!"

But, Thomas was doubtful and said, "I won't believe it until I see the nail marks in his hands and touch his wounds myself."

A week later, the disciples were again all gathered together in the house, and this time Thomas was with them. They had locked the door because they were still afraid of the Jewish leaders coming to arrest them, too.

Suddenly, there in front of them stood Jesus. "Peace be with you," he said. And then he turned to Thomas and showed him his hands. "Look, Thomas, here are my wounds. Come close and touch them."

Thomas was overjoyed to see his master. "My Lord and my God!" he cried out, and he felt very ashamed that he had not had more faith.

Then Jesus told him, "You have believed because you have seen me. God will give a special blessing to those who believe and trust in me, even though they have not seen me with their own eyes."

A while later, Peter, James, John and some of the other disciples went out fishing on the Sea of Galilee. All night long they fished, but they caught nothing.

As the first light of dawn appeared, they saw in the distance a man standing on the beach. He waved at them and called out, "Friends, have you caught any fish?"

"No, they answered, "we haven't caught a thing!"

The stranger shouted back to them, "Throw your net on the right side of the boat and you'll find some."

So they did. Suddenly, the net grew very heavy. In fact, it was so full of fish they could not lift the net on to the boat.

Then John realised who it was calling to them from the shore. "It's the Lord!" he told Peter. As soon as Peter heard these words, he jumped into the water and swam towards the beach. The other disciples followed in the boat, towing the large catch behind them.

On the shore, Jesus had made a small fire, and was cooking some fish for their breakfast. "Bring me some of the ones you have just caught," he called. "We'll need some more."

So, Peter climbed on board the boat and dragged the net ashore.

The disciples counted as one hundred and fifty-three large, silvery fish spilled out on to the sand. It was an enormous catch and yet it had not torn the net at all.

They all sat down together happily, and Jesus shared out the breakfast between them.

The Ascension

After Jesus and his disciples had breakfasted together on the shore, Jesus took Peter to one side.

"Do you love me, Peter?" he asked the disciple.

Peter remembered how he had disowned Jesus, and felt embarrassed and ashamed. "Yes, Lord," he answered. "You know that I love you."

But again Jesus asked, "Peter, do you really love me?"

Peter was hurt that Jesus should have to ask him again but, once more, he answered, "Yes, Lord. You know that I love you."

Jesus asked Peter the same question a third time, and Peter again gave him the same answer. "Lord, you know everything. You *know* that I love you!"

"Then I have an important job for you," said Jesus. "When I am gone, I want you to look after all my followers."

Jesus had asked Peter the same question three times, just as Peter had disowned him three times. Jesus wanted to show Peter that he had forgiven him and that he would trust Peter as his disciple once more.

During the forty days after he had risen from the dead, Jesus appeared to his disciples many times. Each time, he spoke to them about the kingdom of God.

On one occasion, when Jesus was eating with them, he said, "When I have gone, don't leave Jerusalem, but wait for the gift my Father promised to give you. My cousin, John, baptized people with water but, in a few days' time, you will be baptized with the Holy Spirit."

The disciples asked him, "Lord, has the time come for you to rule over your kingdom?" They hoped Jesus would stay and be crowned king.

"God will decide when it is time for that to happen," Jesus told them. "Meanwhile, when the Holy Spirit comes on you, you will receive power. My Father is giving you this power so that you can go into the world and preach forgiveness to all the nations of the earth. Baptize those who repent and want to follow me. Teach them to obey everything I commanded you. Heal the sick just as I have done."

Then, Jesus said to his disciples, "Don't ever forget that, although you can't see me, I am always with you."

After he had said this, Jesus lifted up his hands to bless the apostles. And, as he blessed them, he was taken up to heaven and disappeared from their sight.

While the disciples continued to stare upwards, two men like angels appeared on either side of them. "Men of Galilee, why are you looking up at the sky?" they said. "Jesus has been taken from you now but, one day, he will come back in the same way as he went to heaven."

The Holy Spirit comes

Fifty days after the Passover, the time when Jesus was crucified, the Jews celebrate Pentecost. This is their harvest festival, when they thank God for the first ripe crops and remember God giving the ten commandments to Moses on Mount Sinai. Just as for the Passover, many visitors flocked to Jerusalem to meet together and worship.

On this day, the apostles gathered together, waiting for the Holy Spirit to come. Once again, there were twelve of them, as Judas Iscariot had been replaced by a man called Matthias.

Suddenly, a sound like the blowing of a strong wind came from heaven and filled the house where they were. Then a small flame appeared over the head of each apostle.

As this happened, the apostles were filled with the most wonderful feeling. It was the same sort of sensation they experienced when they talked with Jesus. They felt warmth, strength and a great feeling of joy surging through their bodies. The Holy Spirit had come to live in them, and now they knew and felt Jesus with them all the time.

At the same time, the twelve apostles found that they were able to speak languages they had never learned, or even heard before. They were so filled with joy and love that they laughed and sang and praised God out loud.

Peter speaks to the People

The people close to the house heard these strange happenings, and listened to the apostles singing and praying. A small crowd gathered outside. Amongst them were Jews from different parts of the world, who had come to Jerusalem for the festival.

The apostles came out of the house and began to preach about God. More and more people flocked to listen. Amongst them were Jews from as far away as Africa, Greece and Arabia. All of them were amazed. "Aren't these the men from Galilee?" they asked each other. "How can we hear them talking about the wonders of God, each in our own language?"

But there were others in the crowd who scoffed. "They're talking gibberish!" they said. "They must be drunk."

When Peter heard them say that, he decided it was time to explain. He stood up in front of the crowd, and called out loudly to attract their attention. "Listen carefully, all of you!" he shouted. "These men aren't drunk, as some of you seem to think. It's only nine o' clock in the morning. It's far too early to have been drinking wine!"

Peter continued, "No. Listen, men of Israel. Many years ago, the prophet Joel foretold a time when God would pour out his Holy Spirit on his children. Well, that is what has happened today! God sent you Jesus of Nazareth who, through God, performed great miracles amongst you. This man was given to you by God but, led on by wicked men, you all agreed to have him put to death."

"But, although it seemed like an evil plot, this was all meant to happen. The Lord planned that Jesus should die. He died for our sins. Now God has raised him from the dead because it is impossible for death to kill the Son of God, whom the Lord sent to you as the Messiah, the promised King. He has returned to his Father, and God has poured out the Holy Spirit so that you can all hear and understand."

The crowd listened to everything Peter said. Then they became quiet and thoughtful. Many of them were frightened and ashamed that they had agreed to the death of the Messiah, who was sent by God.

"What can we do?" they asked Peter.

"If you are really sorry, ask God to forgive you and put your trust in Jesus. Come and be baptized and washed clean of all your sins, and you will receive the Holy Spirit, too."

Many of the people truly believed Peter's words, and asked to be baptized. They felt the love of God flow through them, and became followers of Jesus Christ. These people soon told others what had happened, and how they felt. By the end of the day, three thousand people had become believers.

The Early Church

The new believers spent time listening to the apostles' teaching. With the power of the Holy Spirit, they did many miraculous things, so each day more and more people turned to Jesus, and the numbers of believers grew.

One afternoon, Peter and John set off to the temple to pray. On their way, they passed through an entrance to the temple, called the Beautiful Gate. Sitting by the gate, there was a crippled man begging for money. All his life, he had been unable to walk and, each day, the man's friends brought him to the temple, so that he could ask for help from those who went by.

As Peter and John went through the gate, the beggar called out, "Got anything to spare for a poor cripple?"

The apostles stopped and stared at the man. "Look at us," said Peter. And the man looked up at them, expectantly.

Then Peter said to the cripple, "I don't have any money to give, but I do have something else to offer you. In the name of Jesus Christ of Nazareth, I command you to stand up and walk."

Peter took the beggar by the right hand and helped him up. Immediately, the man felt strength coming into his feet and ankles. He jumped up and began to walk. The beggar was so delighted that he followed the two apostles into the temple courts, leaping for joy and praising God.

Everyone turned to see who was causing such a commotion. They stared in wonder and amazement as they recognised the cripple who had sat for so many years at the temple gate. Now he was jumping about in great excitement.

A crowd gathered round to stare at the man clinging to the two apostles. Peter spoke to them all. "Why are you staring like that? We have not healed him. He has been healed by God, through his son, Jesus. It is faith in Jesus that has made this man well."

Then Peter went on to preach to the people, and told them how the Messiah had died for their sins, and had risen from the dead.

News of what was happening reached the ears of the Pharisees and chief priests. They ordered the temple guards to seize Peter and John, and throw them into prison.

The next day, the Jewish leaders questioned the two apostles about the healing of the crippled beggar. "Who gave you the right to do this?" they asked.

The Holy Spirit gave Peter courage to answer truthfully. "We healed this man in the name of Jesus Christ of Nazareth, whom you crucified, but whom God has raised from the dead," he said.

The chief priests and Pharisees were amazed at Peter's nerve, and also that such an uneducated man could explain himself so well. They knew there was nothing they could do as the beggar stood before them as proof of the healing.

So, they ordered the two apostles not to speak or teach at all using the name of Jesus. But Peter and John replied, "Should we obey you or obey God? We have to speak about Jesus and everything that we have seen and heard."

The Jewish leaders threatened them further, but were forced to let them go free.

Stephen the First Martyr

After that, the apostles continued to preach and teach about Jesus, and the numbers of believers grew even more. As there were so many people to care for, Peter asked the new disciples to choose seven leaders to organise the distribution of the money, and make sure the poor widows had what they needed to live on. This gave the apostles more time to pray and teach people.

One of the seven appointed leaders was a man called Stephen. He had great faith in Jesus and, like the apostles, he also went out and preached. God gave Stephen power to do miracles among the people, and crowds flocked to hear him.

Soon, some of the Jewish leaders heard about Stephen's teaching, and argued against what he said. But Stephen's enemies could not trick him. So, instead they persuaded people to lie and suggest that Stephen was speaking against the prophet Moses, and God.

Stephen was arrested, and brought before the Sanhedrin, the same council of priests and Pharisees who had put Jesus on trial. As they read out the false charges against him, the Jewish leaders saw that Stephen's face was like that of an angel. It was full of joy, goodness and peace.

"Well!" they shouted. "What have you got to say for yourself?"

God gave Stephen courage, and he spoke out bravely and truthfully. He reminded the Jewish leaders that, in the past, all prophets of God had either been ignored or persecuted by people like them.

"You are just like the rest," he said to the members of the council. "In the past, they killed those who predicted the coming of the Messiah. Now you have rejected and murdered the Messiah himself."

When they heard these words, the priests and Pharisees were enraged. But, without any fear, Stephen stood staring upwards. "Look," he said. "I see Jesus, the Son of God, sitting at the right hand of his Father."

At this, the priests and Pharisees gasped in horror and shouted at Stephen, "How dare you speak against God like that!"

They seized him, and dragged him off to a place outside the city walls. There, they picked up boulders and large stones, and began to hurl them at Stephen. A crowd gathered to join in, and among those who watched was a man called Saul. He held the cloaks of the people pelting Stephen with rocks.

In those days, to stone someone to death was a common form of execution. Stephen knew he was going to die. As the sharp, heavy stones cut and wounded him, he whispered, "Lord Jesus, receive my spirit."

A huge boulder hit Stephen on the head and he fell to his knees. "Lord," he cried out, "forgive them for what they are doing."

When he had said this, Stephen lay down on the ground and died. He was the first follower of Jesus to die for his belief.

Paul's Conversion

After Stephen's death, those who believed in Jesus, (or followers of 'the Way' as they were called then) were hunted down and persecuted. Some were put in prison, but many of them fled. The ringleader of the opposition was Saul, the man who had stood by and watched as Stephen was killed.

Saul was a well-educated young man who knew Greek and Latin. His parents were Jews, but he had been born in Tarsus, a town in a Roman province. He had therefore been given Roman citizenship and in his home town was known by his Roman name, Paul.

As well as being clever, Saul was also a very devout Pharisee, and had been taught everything about the Jewish religion by the best teacher in Jerusalem. He was convinced that the followers of Jesus were in the wrong, and that they must be wiped out. Saul travelled everywhere, searching out new believers and arresting them.

One day, Saul and his armed guards set off for the city of Damascus. He had permission from the leaders of the Jewish Council to arrest the followers of 'the Way' who were to be found living there. The journey took nearly a week, but, at last, in the distance, Saul could see the city.

As he travelled along the hot dusty road, a brilliant light flashed around Saul. The light was so dazzling, Saul fell to the ground.

Then he heard a voice saying, "Saul, Saul, why are you persecuting me?"

Saul was trembling in awe at this heavenly light. "Who are you, Lord?" he asked.

"I am Jesus, whom you are persecuting," replied the voice. "Now get up, and go into the city. There you will be told what you must do."

When Saul staggered to his feet, he found he was blind. His soldiers stood there speechless. They had heard a sound, but had not seen anything else at all. So, very slowly, the armed guard led their master into the city. There, they stayed at a house in Straight Street. For three days, Saul was blind and refused to eat or drink.

In Damascus, there was a disciple of Jesus, called Ananias. The Lord spoke to him in a vision, and told him to go to the house in Straight Street, where Saul of Tarsus was staying. "I have told Saul that you will go and pray for him, so that his sight will be restored," Jesus said to Ananias.

The disciple was very worried. "But Lord," he said. "I've heard about Saul. He's the one who arrests all who believe in you."

But Jesus reassured Ananias. "I have chosen this man to be my servant. He will be a great apostle who will preach about me in many countries of the world. Now go to him."

So, Ananias found the house, and went in. He laid his hands on Saul and said, "Brother Saul, the Lord Jesus who appeared to you on the road has sent me here so that you may see again, and be filled with the Holy Spirit."

Immediately, Saul was able to see again. Then Ananias baptized him, and Saul sat down and ate a good meal.

Peter leads the Believers

After Saul had been converted, and was no longer against them, the followers of Jesus could preach and teach in peace for a while. They journeyed far and wide, spreading the good news about the Lord in many different cities.

As Peter was travelling about the country, healing the sick and teaching about Jesus, he came close to the port of Joppa.

In this town, there was a disciple of Jesus, called Tabitha. She was a kind and loving woman who was always generous to the poor. Tabitha was very good at sewing, and had made many clothes for people who could not afford to buy them.

At this time, Tabitha was sick and, one day, she grew so ill, she died. When the other believers heard that Peter was in a nearby town, they sent for him urgently.

When Peter arrived, he found many friends and relations were gathered in the house, weeping. They showed him some of the clothes the kind woman had made for them.

Peter went up to the room where Tabitha lay, and sent everyone away. He knelt down and prayed to Jesus. Then, he turned towards the dead woman and said, "Tabitha, get up!"

Very slowly, Tabitha opened her eyes. When she saw Peter, she sat up. He took her by the hand and helped her to her feet.

Peter called to the believers and others that were there mourning, and presented Tabitha, alive.

News of this event spread throughout Joppa, and many people came to believe in Jesus because of what Peter had done in his name.

Peter stayed for a while in Joppa, at the house of a man called Simon. He was a tanner and, because he worked with animal hides, many Jews considered him 'unclean'. But Jesus had taught his disciples that God did not treat someone as unclean by what they touched or ate. He was more concerned with whether people's thoughts or actions were clean and wholesome.

One day, at about noon, Peter went up to the roof of the house to pray. He was very hungry and was looking forward to his next meal. As Peter sat praying to God, the heat made his eyes heavy, and soon he was fast asleep.

While he slept, Peter had a strange dream, or vision. He saw heaven opening and a large sheet being let down to earth by its four corners. Collected inside the sheet were all the creatures that Jews were forbidden to eat.

Then a voice said, "Get up, Peter. Kill and eat."

Peter was horrified and replied, "Surely not, Lord. I have never eaten anything unclean!"

But the voice answered, "Do not call anything unclean that God has made clean."

The sheet was lowered before Peter three times.

Then Peter woke up, and wondered what the vision meant. He knew that God was trying to explain something. Then he felt God's Spirit saying, "Three men are looking for you, so get up and go downstairs. Do not hesitate to go with them, for I have sent them to you."

God guides and rescues Peter

Standing at the door were men who had been sent by a Roman centurion, called Cornelius. Peter welcomed them in.

"Our master is a good, honest man," they told Peter. "He is respected by all the Jewish people. An angel of God has appeared to Cornelius, and told him to request a visit from you, so that he can listen to your teaching."

Cornelius was a centurion in the Italian regiment in Caesarea. He prayed to God regularly and gave generously to the poor. So God had decided Cornelius should know about Jesus and, as Peter was nearby, this was the perfect opportunity.

In those days, people who were not Jews were called Gentiles. As they did not live according to the strict Jewish rules, the Jews considered the Gentiles 'unclean', and would not invite them into their homes.

Peter now realised that, in the dream, God was trying to tell him that he wanted to welcome the Gentiles as well as the Jews. He invited the centurion's three servants to stay the night and, the next day, he set off with them to the home of Cornelius.

When Peter arrived, the house was full of people who had gathered to listen to him. So, Peter told them all about Jesus.

"I now realise that God has no favourites," said Peter. "He accepts men from every nation who worship and respect him."

As Peter spoke to them, the Holy Spirit came upon them all, just as on the day of Pentecost. The Jews who were with Peter were astonished that God had blessed and welcomed the Gentiles, and that they, too, could speak in different languages. Through this, the apostles learned that Jesus had come to be the Messiah for everyone, not just the Jews.

Not long after this had happened, King Herod Agrippa became king in Judea, and decided to persecute the followers of Jesus. He had the apostle James put to death, and arrested Peter, intending to have him tried after the Passover.

Peter was thrown into a dark dungeon, bound in chains, and guarded by four soldiers, day and night. All the time he was there, the other believers prayed to God for Peter's protection. Despite all that faced him, the night before his trial, Peter slept soundly.

Suddenly, a brilliant light lit up the prison, and an angel of God appeared beside Peter. He had to shake Peter hard to wake him. "Quick, get up!" he said to the apostle, and the chains fell loose from Peter's wrists. The angel told Peter to get dressed and follow him.

Peter thought he was dreaming when the angel led him past rows of sleeping guards, out of the prison, and through the huge iron gate leading to the city. Once he was out of danger the angel left Peter, and he realised he was awake.

Then Peter knew that the Lord had rescued him from his enemy, Herod.

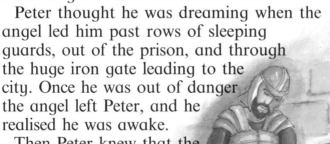

Paul, the Apostle to the Gentiles

After Saul had been converted, he was a changed man. In Damascus, instead of persecuting the new believers, he joined them and preached about Jesus all over the city.

The Jews who knew Saul well could not believe it. They were angry with him, and planned to kill him. His enemies kept watch at the gates of the city, so he could not leave. But the believers heard about the plot, and they helped Saul to escape by lowering him down the steep city walls in a basket.

When he reached Jerusalem, Saul tried to join the disciples there, but they were afraid of him, and thought it was a trick.

A disciple, called Barnabas, knew about Saul's vision of Jesus, so he went with Saul to the apostles and told them all that had happened. Then they welcomed Saul, and he joined them, preaching and teaching in the city of Jerusalem.

As he was so well-educated, Saul was able to discuss what he believed in Greek to the Grecian Jews. But they grew angry at what they heard, and they, too, tried to kill Saul. After that, the apostles sent him to Tarsus (where he was born), for his own safety. There he stayed for some years, preaching and teaching about Jesus.

Meanwhile, Barnabas had travelled to a place called Antioch, where a great many people had become followers of 'the Way'. As Antioch was quite near to Tarsus, Barnabas asked Saul to join him. For a year, the two friends taught large numbers of people in Antioch. The believers were called 'Christians', and Saul became known by his Roman name, Paul.

One day, God made it clear to the Christians in Antioch that he wanted Paul and Barnabas to preach to people in other lands.

So, the believers prayed for the two men, and they set out first for the island of Cyprus. There, Paul and Barnabas preached about Jesus in the Jewish synagogues. Although some people opposed them, many listened and were converted.

From Cyprus, the two apostles set sail for the mainland north of the island, which we now call Turkey. There, they taught the Jews that Jesus was the Messiah. Many Jews were angry at what they heard, so Paul and Barnabas preached to the Gentiles instead. They welcomed the apostles, and many became Christians.

This made the Jews hate the apostles even more, and Paul and Barnabas were often threatened or beaten up. When the two apostles heard that their enemies were planning to stone them, they left that town, and fled to a place called Lystra.

While they were in Lystra, preaching and teaching about God, Paul saw a man with crippled feet, who had been lame from birth. So, in the name of Jesus, Paul healed the man.

When the people saw this, they were amazed. They thought that Paul and Barnabas were the Greek gods, Zeus and Hermes, who had come down to earth in human form. They brought garlands of flowers and animals to sacrifice to them. The apostles finally convinced the people that they were messengers from the true God. Then they set off for Antioch to report back to the church there.

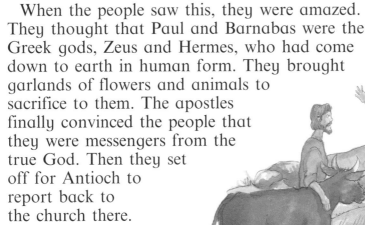

Paul's Journey to Europe

After Paul had been back in Antioch for a while, he decided it was time to visit the new Christians in Cyprus and Turkey to encourage them, and strengthen the churches there. So, Barnabas and Mark went to Cyprus, and Paul set off for Syria and Turkey, accompanied by Silas.

One night, while he was in Troas, Paul had a very vivid dream. In it, a man from Macedonia was standing in front of him, begging him to come to his land and help. So, Paul felt God was telling him to head across the sea to the part of the world we now call Europe.

Once in Macedonia, Paul and his companion headed for the capital city of Philippi. As they were preaching outside the city, a businesswoman, called Lydia, listened to them and became a Christian. Once she and all the members of her family had been baptized, she invited Paul and his friend to stay at her house.

Each day, when the men went out to preach, they were met by a slave girl, who made money for her owners by telling fortunes. In a strange voice, the girl kept calling out loudly, "These men are the servants of the Most High God who are telling you the way to be saved!"

Paul knew that the girl was possessed by an evil spirit, which controlled her and gave her the power to predict the future. So, he said to the spirit, "In the name of Jesus Christ, I command you to come out of her!" The girl immediately stopped ranting, but she also lost her ability to tell fortunes, too.

When her owners discovered what Paul had done, they were furious, and had the disciples arrested. Straightaway, Paul and Silas were taken away to be flogged, and thrown into prison.

"Guard these Christians carefully!" the officer ordered the jailer. So, he took the prisoners and fastened their feet in stocks.

Despite all that they had suffered, that night in their dungeon Paul and Silas prayed to God, and sang hymns of praise. The other prisoners listened in amazement. Then, at midnight, there was a violent earthquake. The foundations of the prison shook, the doors flew open, and everyone's chains came loose.

When the jailer woke up, he was horrified as he thought the prisoners had escaped. He knew he would be blamed, so he drew out his sword ready to kill himself. "Don't harm yourself!" shouted Paul. "We're all here."

The jailer went in to where Paul and Silas were sitting. "Sirs," he said, "what can I do to be saved?"

Then Paul answered, "Believe in the Lord Jesus, and you and your family will be saved."

So, the jailer and his household were baptized. He took Paul and Silas, washed their wounds and gave them a good meal.

The next day, Paul and Silas were released from prison. The magistrates were worried when they discovered they had flogged a Roman citizen without a trial. The two friends said 'goodbye' to Lydia, left Philippi, and continued on their travels.

Paul's Third Journey

Some time later, Paul set off from Antioch again. During this third journey, he spent over two years in Ephesus, which was famous for its beautiful temple, built in honour of the Greek goddess, Artemis.

To begin with, Paul went to the Jewish synagogue to preach but, as the Jews there opposed him, he spoke to the crowds in a large lecture hall. The local people flocked to listen to Paul, and God gave him the power to do great miracles and healings, so that many of the Gentiles believed and became Christians.

When people became Christians, they stopped practising anything to do with magic, and no longer believed in the goddess, Artemis. Soon, this caused a problem for the local silversmiths, who made little models of Artemis to sell outside the temple. One of these, a man called Demetrius, called a meeting of the craftsmen and traders of that area.

"We have all made a good living from our work until now," he said, "but this fellow, Paul, is ruining our trade! On top of that, he is turning everyone away from our beautiful goddess, Artemis."

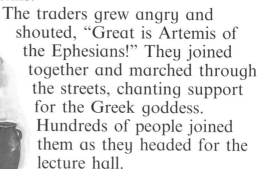

The traders grew angry and shouted, "Great is Artemis of the Ephesians!" They joined together and marched through the streets, chanting support for the Greek goddess. Hundreds of people joined them as they headed for the lecture hall.

The local disciples had heard the uproar, and warned Paul not to appear before the crowds. Many of the people did not know why they were chanting – they had just joined the noisy mob, looking for trouble. Finally, the city clerk quietened the crowd, and sent them all home.

After that, Paul decided it would be better for the new Christians if he left Ephesus. So, he travelled on through Macedonia and Greece, returning once again to Troas. There, the new believers crowded into a room on the third storey of a house to listen to Paul speak. The room became so stuffy that a young man, called Eutychus, nodded off to sleep. Unfortunately, he was sitting on the window sill and fell out of the open window, crashing down to the ground. "He's dead!" gasped the people below.

But Paul rushed down to the young man and said, "Don't worry, he's alive!" The young man breathed again, and his friends took him home.

Next, Paul travelled in the direction of Jerusalem. He was eager to help and encourage the Christians who were living in poverty there. On his travels, Paul had collected money to give to the believers in Jerusalem, so he was keen to get this to them as soon as possible.

One day, while he was staying in Caesarea, a prophet, called Agabus, gave Paul a warning. He took Paul's belt and used it to tie his own hands and feet. "This is what will happen to you if you return to Jerusalem," said Agabus. "God has told me that the Jews in Jerusalem will have you arrested."

Paul listened, but he was not going to change his mind. He said, "If necessary, I am ready to die in Jerusalem for the name of the Lord Jesus."

Paul is arrested

So Paul made his way to the city of
Jerusalem, and the Jewish Christians there
gave him a warm welcome. But they also
warned the apostle that he might be in danger.

Paul was determined to carry on teaching
about Jesus, so he went to the temple and began
to preach. Some of the leading Jews from Asia
noticed Paul and called out, "Fellow Jews, help
us! This is the man who teaches a new religion
which breaks God's law. He even brings
Gentiles into the temple!"

People came running from all directions. The
crowd seized Paul, dragged him from the temple
area and began to beat him up. The commander
of the Roman troops heard the commotion and
immediately sent soldiers to control the riot. The
guards arrested Paul and bound him in chains.

"Who is this man?" asked the commander.
"What's he done?" But he could get no sense
from the mob. The soldiers had to carry Paul
over the heaving crowd, who kept chanting,
"Away with him! Kill him!"

The Romans took Paul back to the barracks,
and were just about to flog him when Paul told
them that he was a Roman citizen. When he
heard this, the commander immediately treated
Paul with respect and allowed him to appear
before the Jewish Council to plead his case.

When they learned that Paul had been a
Pharisee, some of the Jewish leaders listened
carefully and found him innocent. But
others disagreed, and soon there was more
trouble. Once again, the Roman soldiers
took Paul back to the barracks.

After this, some of the Jews plotted to kill Paul, but his nephew heard about it and warned his uncle. When the Roman commander was informed, he decided it was time to have Paul removed from the city. So, one night, protected by hundreds of Roman soldiers, the apostle was secretly smuggled out of Jerusalem and taken to the Roman governor at Caesarea.

There Paul remained a prisoner for several years. During this time, he was brought before different governors to defend his case, but each time this happened nothing was ever settled. Eventually, Paul used his right as a Roman citizen to appeal to the Emperor, himself. He knew that this was what God wanted as, one night, God had told Paul, "Be brave. Just as you have spoken about me in Jerusalem, so you must also speak about me in Rome."

Paul was handed over to Julius, a Roman centurion in charge of prisoners heading for the capital in Italy. The disciple, Luke, decided to accompany Paul, so he, too, boarded the ship and they set sail. At first, the weather was good and the sea was calm. But after a while, the wind changed and it was difficult for the ship to make any progress. Paul warned Julius, "This voyage will be disastrous for all of us if we continue in this weather." The captain of the ship was eager to transport his cargo, however, so Julius decided to ignore Paul's warning and travel on.

Shipwrecked!

As they sailed close to Crete, a great hurricane blew up and the ship was battered by the most terrible storm. The wind howled and raged around the little ship and huge waves crashed down on to the deck. The crew lashed the lifeboat to the deck and, to lighten the vessel, they began to throw the cargo and equipment overboard.

The storm raged on for many days. It was so fierce the sailors could not tell whether it was night or day. The passengers and crew were terrified and exhausted, and had given up all hope of being saved. Then Paul gathered everyone together and said, "If you had listened to my warning, you would have been spared all this damage and loss. But don't be afraid, last night God spoke to me. He has promised me that no one will drown."

Two weeks later, the ship was still being tossed about the sea. But, one night, the sailors sensed that they were close to land. So, they took soundings and discovered that the water was shallower. The crew dropped anchor, secretly planning to escape from the ship in the lifeboat as soon as it was light.

But Paul knew what they were up to, and warned the Roman centurion, "Unless those men stay with the ship, you cannot be saved." So, the soldiers cut the ropes that held the lifeboat and it fell away into the sea.

Just before dawn, Paul encouraged everyone to eat. "For two weeks you have been fighting the weather and have hardly eaten. Now you need to build up your strength for what lies ahead. God has promised that we will all survive." Then he took some food, thanked God for it and ate.

At daybreak, they saw a bay with a sandy beach, so they cut loose the anchors and hoped the ship would run aground on the shore. But the ship hit a sandbank and started to break up.

Julius, the centurion, shouted out orders. "Those who can swim, jump overboard! The rest of you cling to planks of wood and head for the beach." So, that is what they did, and all two hundred and seventy-six people reached land safely.

The castaways discovered they were on the island of Malta. The people who lived there were very friendly and built a fire to warm the cold, wet survivors. The Roman governor lived near to the coast, and he welcomed everyone into his villa, where they stayed for three days.

The governor's father was seriously ill in bed, so Paul asked if he could help. First, he prayed to God, then the apostle laid his hands on the old man and he was healed. When news of this spread, all the sick people on the island came to Paul and were cured. Then the islanders helped the castaways and, when it was time to set sail again, they gave them supplies for the voyage.

Three months later, the prisoners and crew continued their journey. Finally, after all his adventures, Paul arrived safely in Rome.

The Letters of Paul

The Christians in Rome gave Paul a warm welcome and, as he awaited trial, the Romans allowed him to rent a house which was guarded by a soldier.

Although he was not allowed to go out, many people flocked to Paul's home to listen to him teach about Jesus. From morning till night, Paul talked to them and answered their questions. At first, he invited the Jews to hear him, but they did not want to believe that Jesus was the Messiah. So then Paul preached the gospel to the Gentiles.

The apostle spent two years waiting to appear before the Emperor and, during this time, he continued to write letters to the Christians in the places he had visited on his journeys. He wanted to keep on encouraging these people, even though he could no longer visit them.

Sometimes he wrote personal messages to friends such as Timothy, and Lydia, the businesswoman who sent him money. In other letters, he gave instructions about how the new Christians should lead their lives. These letters still guide Christians today.

When Paul wrote to the Philippians (people of Philippi), he told them how his being in prison had helped to spread the gospel even more. Paul wanted these new Christians to understand that, if Jesus was the most important thing in their lives, they would always have joy and something good would always come out of all the bad things that happened to them.

Paul encouraged the Philippians to look after each other well, and not to be selfish. He wrote, "Do everything without complaining and arguing... also, do not worry about anything, but be thankful and pray to God about your problems and needs."

The apostle wrote to the Colossians reminding them not to be swayed by ideas from other religions. If they believed in Christ, they were to stick to the truth taught by Jesus and not make their own version of Christianity.

He told them not to be greedy or lie to one another, nor to lose their temper or swear. Instead, he told them that God wanted Christians to be patient, kind, humble and gentle. They were to forgive each other for the wrong things they did and, above all, they were to be loving to everyone.

When Paul wrote to the Ephesians (people of Ephesus), he told them that all Christians are bound together by what they believe in. They serve one Master. He is the head and those that believe in him are the many parts of the body. Although Christians are all different, they must use their various talents for the good of each other, and they must be loving and forgiving to their fellow believers. Husbands and wives should be kind and loving to each other, and children should obey their parents.

Finally, he warned them that they were now involved in the battle of good against evil. They needed always to pray. He wrote, "Put on the whole armour of God, so that you can take your stand against the Devil's schemes."

The Letters of James and Peter

Paul was not the only leader to write letters to encourage and teach the new believers. James, the brother of John, and Peter both wrote to Christians in the early church. James became a believer after he saw Jesus had risen from the dead, and he later became a leader in the church in Jerusalem.

James wrote to all Christians, stressing how important it was to show you really believed in Jesus by your actions. "It is no good saying that you are a Christian unless you behave in the way that Jesus taught. Everyone should be quick to listen, slow to speak and slow to become angry," wrote James. "It is important to be careful what you say. Christians should not gossip or say anything they may regret later... nor should they judge each other's behaviour."

Another thing James felt strongly about was being snobbish. "Christians are to treat everyone equally, however rich or poor, whatever race or colour." He also warned people against becoming too interested in money. "The rich think their money can protect them, and it stops them from drawing close to God for their needs. Christians are to turn to God for everything."

He told them, "If you are in trouble, you should pray. If you are happy, praise God. If you are sick, ask the leaders of the church to pray over you and anoint you with oil in the name of the Lord... if you have sinned, God will forgive you. So, tell each other your sins and pray for each other. God hears your prayers."

Peter had become leader of the twelve apostles after Jesus had ascended to heaven. Although he was not educated, he also wrote letters to believers scattered everywhere. Peter probably also wrote from Rome, at the time when the Emperor Nero began his cruel persecution of the Christians.

Peter tried to prepare believers for a time when they might suffer for their faith. "Do not be surprised if you have to face all kinds of trials, which will test your faith... remember, Jesus Christ also suffered terrible pain when he died for us. Christians can be glad, even in times of great hardship, because this is when our belief is really tested, and we can share in the suffering that Jesus experienced."

"You belong to God," wrote Peter. "Be holy, and do not be tempted to do wrong things. Live such good lives that those who are not Christians will notice how God's people are different from others."

"Be gentle and respect other people, no matter how harshly they may treat you. If you suffer for doing good, God will bless you. Those who killed Jesus hurled insults at him, but he did not shout back. They beat and flogged him, but he said nothing. They accused him of things he did not do, but still he remained silent. We must try to be like him."

"After you have suffered, God will restore you and make you strong again. So, pray to him and he will care for you."

John's Vision of the Future

Many years went by, and the Christians did suffer greatly for their belief in Jesus. Some of them were put to death and others were imprisoned.

When he was very old, the apostle John was forced to live in exile on the island of Patmos, probably working in the island's quarries. John often thought back to the time of Jesus' ascension. The angels had told the apostles, "This same Jesus, who has been taken from you into heaven, will come back in the same way you have seen him go." Like all other Christians, John hoped that Jesus would come back in his lifetime to overcome the evil in the world. The Christian church wanted something to happen to encourage them to stand firm.

Over a period of time, God gave John a spectacular vision of the future, which he wrote down. In the Bible, this book is called 'Revelation', because God revealed to John, by means of images and symbols, what was going to happen to the world.

In the vision, Jesus appeared to John in great glory, and gave him messages for each of the seven churches of Asia. Then John was given a marvellous glimpse of heaven. Encircled by a great rainbow, God sat on his throne shining out with the radiance of a million sparkling jewels. In his right hand, God held a scroll, which was sealed with seven seals. An angel called out in a loud voice, "Who is worthy to break the seals and open the scroll?"

There was only one person considered good enough to open the scroll and reveal God's plan for the future. That was Jesus. When Jesus appeared in front of John, it was in the form of a lamb. This was because he had been sacrificed to save the world. As Jesus took the scroll, thousands and thousands of angels encircled the throne singing, "Worthy is the lamb who was slain to receive power and honour and glory and praise!"

Jesus broke the first seal and began to unroll the events of the future. As John listened, he was reassured. Although Satan, the enemy of God, has spread evil over the world, and good people suffer, God is still in control. Jesus overcame evil by dying and returning to live for ever. He will come back again and the world will be different. Satan will be destroyed, the world as we know it will end, and Jesus will bring a new world that is fresh, beautiful and good.

God told John, "For those who believe in me, I am going to make everything new, and they will live for ever. But those who murder, lie, steal and do other wicked things must beware. Unless they change and ask for forgiveness, they will be sent away from me and suffer for ever."

John wrote, "Then I saw a new heaven and a new earth, and I heard a loud voice from the throne saying, 'Now God will live with men. They will be his people and he will wipe away all tears. There will be no more death or grief or crying or pain, because all these will have passed away.'"

"I am coming soon," Jesus promised. How Christians long for that day!

Who's Who in the Stories

Aaron   The brother of Moses. He was Moses' spokesman when he asked Pharaoh to let the children of Israel leave Egypt. *Pages 47-49, 52, 53, 60.*

Abel   The second son of Adam and Eve, and the brother of Cain. *Pages 14-16.*

Abraham   The father of the nation of Israel. He was a man of great faith who was always totally obedient to God. *Pages 22-27, 32, 47, 60.*

Absalom   One of the sons of King David. *Pages 108-112.*

Adam   The first man, created by God, and the father of Cain and Abel. *Pages 13,14.*

Ahab   The king of Israel at the time of the prophet, Elijah, and the husband of Jezebel. *Pages 124-126, 128, 130, 131, 136, 138.*

Amos   A prophet of God from Judah. He was sent by God to speak to the people of Israel. *Pages 138, 139.*

Ananias   The Christian who prayed for Saul in Damascus after he was blinded. *Page 291.*

Andrew   One of Jesus' disciples. He was a fisherman and the brother of Peter. *Pages 191, 195, 207.*

Barnabas   A Christian from Cyprus who travelled with Paul on his missionary journey from Antioch. *Pages 216, 217, 218.*

Bathsheba   The wife of King David, and mother of King Solomon. *Pages 106-108, 112, 113.*

Belshazzar   The wicked king of Babylon who was warned by God through writing on a wall. His kingdom was overthrown by the Persians. *Page 156.*

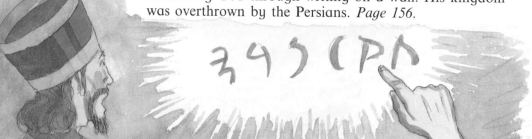

Benjamin   The youngest son of Jacob and Rachel, and the brother of Joseph. *Pages 40-42, 84.*

Boaz   A farmer from Bethlehem who married Ruth and became the ancestor of David. *Pages 78, 79.*

Caiaphas   The high priest in Jerusalem at the time of Jesus' arrest, trial and crucifixion. *Pages 255, 264, 266.*

Cain   The first son of Adam and Eve. He killed his own brother, Abel. *Pages 14-16.*

Cleopas   One of the two people whom Jesus appeared to on the road to Emmaus. *Pages 276, 277.*

Daniel   A great prophet of God. He was among the Jews in exile in Babylon. He rose to an important position as God gave him the power to interpret dreams. *Pages 150-152, 154-159.*

David   The shepherd boy from Bethlehem, who killed the giant Goliath and became king of Israel. He founded the royal line from which Jesus was born. *Pages 79, 90-114, 116, 120, 122, 145.*

Delilah   A beautiful Philistine woman who tricked Samson into revealing the secret of his strength. *Page 73.*

Devil   (also known as Satan) The enemy of God, who brought evil and sin into the world. *Pages 13, 190, 194, 227, 307.*

Eli   The high priest who looked after and taught the prophet Samuel when he was a boy. *Pages 80-85.*

Elijah   A great prophet of Israel who had a contest with the priests of Baal to prove the power of the only true God. *Pages 124-129, 131-134, 136, 138, 188, 222, 224.*

Elisha   The man who followed Elijah as the prophet of God. *Pages 129, 132-137.*

Elizabeth   The wife of Zechariah, mother of John the Baptist and cousin of Mary, the mother of Jesus. *Pages 172-175.*

Esau   The son of Isaac and Rebekah. He was tricked by his twin brother, Jacob, into selling his birthright. *Pages 28-31, 35, 36.*

Esther   The Jewish woman who married Xerxes, the king of Persia. She prevented the massacre of the Jews in exile. *Pages 164-169.*

Eve   The first woman, created by God, and mother of Cain and Abel. *Pages 13, 14.*

Ezekiel   A prophet of God in exile in Babylon. He had a vision of hope for the people of Israel. *Pages 160, 161.*

Gabriel   The angel sent by God to announce the birth of Jesus to Mary, and the birth of John the Baptist to Elizabeth. *Pages 173, 174, 177.*

Gideon   A young man who, with God's help and only a few soldiers, rescued Israel from the Midianites. *Pages 68, 69, 76.*

Goliath   The Philistine giant killed by the young shepherd boy, David. *Pages 92-96, 98.*

Haman   The wicked prime minister of Xerxes, king of Persia. His plan to kill all the Jews in exile was stopped by Queen Esther. *Pages 166-169.*

Herod the Great   The king of Judea at the time of Jesus' birth. He ordered the massacre of all the boys aged under two in Bethlehem. *Pages 172, 180-182, 184, 185, 204.*

Hosea   A prophet of God from Israel. He warned the people about turning away from God. *Pages 138, 139.*

Isaac   The son of Abraham and Sarah, and the father of Esau and Jacob. He married Rebekah. *Pages 23-32, 47.*

Isaiah   A great prophet of God from Israel. He warned the people about turning away from God. *Pages 144, 145.*

Jacob   The son of Isaac and Rebekah, and brother of Esau. He married Leah and Rachel, and was the father of the twelve tribes of Israel. *Pages 28-37, 40-42, 47.*

James   The name of two of Jesus' disciples. *Pages 191, 203, 224, 225, 260, 278, 295, 308.*

Jeremiah   The prophet who foretold the destruction of Jerusalem. *Pages 146-148, 160.*

Jesus Christ   The Son of God and the Messiah whose coming was foretold by the great Old Testament prophets. He was the only sinless human being, who was put to death but rose to life again. He was sent by God to rescue people from sin and death and give them the promise of 'eternal life' in heaven. Those who believe in Christ are called Christians. *Pages 174-282, 311.*

Jezebel   The wicked queen who marrried King Ahab and introduced the worship of Baal into Israel. She organised the death of Naboth. *Pages 124-126, 128-131, 138.*

Jochebed   The mother of Moses, Aaron and Miriam. *Pages 44, 45.*

John   The brother of James, and one of Jesus' disciples. He was the writer of the fourth gospel. *Pages 191, 203, 224, 225, 260, 271, 274, 275, 278-280, 286, 287, 308, 310, 311.*

John the Baptist   The cousin of Jesus who was a prophet of God. He prepared people for Jesus' coming. *Pages 172, 173, 188, 189, 204-206, 222.*

Jonah   The prophet who disobeyed God and was swallowed by a whale. After this, he did as he was told and preached to the people of Ninevah. *Pages 140-143.*

Jonathan   The son of King Saul, and a close friend of David. *Pages 87, 88.*

Joseph The favourite son of Jacob. He was sold into slavery in Egypt by his jealous brothers. With God's help, he rose to great power and saved Egypt and the Israelites from starvation. *Pages 36-42.*

Joseph The husband of Mary, the mother of Jesus. *Pages 174-177, 179, 182-187.*

Joseph of Arimathea The rich Jewish leader who provided the tomb for Jesus' burial. *Page 272.*

Joshua The brave man who led the Israelites into the Promised Land after Moses' death. By obeying God's orders, he conquered the city of Jericho. *Pages 62-68.*

Judas Iscariot The disciple who betrayed Jesus. *Pages 191, 248, 255, 256, 259, 260, 262, 266, 282.*

Laban The brother of Rebekah, who tricked Jacob into marrying Leah before he could marry Rachel. *Pages 27, 31, 33, 34, 35.*

Lazarus The brother of Mary and Martha. He was a friend of Jesus, who raised him from the dead. *Pages 242-245, 248, 250.*

Luke A companion of Paul on some of his missionary journeys. He wrote one of the four gospels. *Page 303.*

Mark The companion of Paul and Barnabas, and writer of one of the four gospels. *Page 298.*

Martha The sister of Mary and Lazarus, and a close friend of Jesus. *Pages 242-245, 248, 249.*

Mary The mother of Jesus, and wife of Joseph. *Pages 174-179, 182-187, 192, 271.*

Mary The sister of Martha and Lazarus, and a close friend of Jesus. *Pages 242-245, 248, 249.*

Mary Magdalene   The first person to see Jesus raised from the dead. *Pages 272, 275.*

Matthew   A tax-collector who became one of Jesus' disciples. He wrote the first gospel. *Page 191.*

Michal   The daughter of King Saul, and wife of David. *Pages 97, 102, 103.*

Mordecai   The cousin and protector of Queen Esther who was one of the Jews in exile in Babylon. *Pages 164-169.*

Moses   The prophet who led the Israelites out of slavery in Egypt through years of wandering in the desert until they were allowed to enter the Promised Land. God gave Moses the ten commandments on Mount Sinai. *Pages 44-64, 129, 132, 149, 220, 224, 228.*

Naaman   The army general who had leprosy and was healed by Elisha. *Pages 136, 137.*

Naboth   A farmer who was killed for his vineyard by King Ahab after a plot by Queen Jezebel. *Pages 130, 131.*

Naomi   The mother-in-law of Ruth, who married Boaz, an ancestor of David and Jesus. *Pages 76-79.*

Nathan   The prophet who gave God's word to King David and helped to put King Solomon on the throne. *Pages 104, 105, 107, 108, 112, 113.*

Nebuchadnezzar   The powerful king of Babylon who destroyed Jerusalem and took the people of Judah into exile. *Pages 148-155, 160, 162.*

Nehemiah   The Jewish cupbearer of the Persian king, Artaxerxes, who let Nehemiah return to Jerusalem to help with the rebuilding of the city. *Pages 162-164.*

Noah   The man who, with his family, was saved from death in the great flood by God telling him to build an ark. *Pages 16-19, 22.*

Paul/Saul A Jew who persecuted Christians before his conversion to Christ on the road to Damascus. He became a great Christian leader and apostle to the Gentiles (non-Jewish people), and wrote many letters to encourage and guide new Christians. *Pages 289-292, 296-308.*

Peter (also known as Simon Peter) One of Jesus' disciples and a close friend of Jesus. He became a leader of the early Christian church. *Pages 191, 195, 203, 211, 222-225, 257, 259, 260, 262-265, 274, 275, 278-280, 284-288, 292-295, 308, 309.*

Pharaoh The name given to an Egyptian king. *Pages 38, 39, 44-46, 48-51, 53, 54.*

Pontius Pilate The Roman governor of Judea who allowed the Jews to crucify Jesus. *Pages 266, 267, 272, 273.*

Potiphar The Egyptian official for whom Joseph worked in Egypt. His wife caused Joseph to be put in prison. *Page 38.*

Queen of Sheba The rich queen who heard so much about King Solomon that she travelled from her land to see him. *Pages 118, 119.*

Rachel The second, favourite wife of Jacob, and mother of Joseph and Benjamin. She was Laban's daughter and Leah's sister. *Pages 33, 34, 36.*

Rebekah The wife of Isaac, and mother of Esau and Jacob. *Pages 26-31.*

Rehoboam The son of Solomon who caused the kingdom of Israel to be split into two. *Page 123.*

Ruth The Moabite daughter-in-law of Naomi, who married Boaz in Bethlehem and became the great-grandmother of King David. *Pages 76-79.*

Samson A very strong Israelite man who fought against the Philistines in the time of the Judges. *Pages 70-76.*

Samuel   The great prophet and judge of Israel who anointed King Saul and King David, Israel's first two kings. *Pages 80-89.*

Sarah   The wife of Abraham, and mother of Isaac. *Pages 22, 24.*

Satan   Another name for the Devil, the enemy of God, who brought evil into the world. *Pages 190, 223, 311.*

Saul   The first king of Israel, and father of Jonathan. *Pages 84-90, 92-94, 96-102, 104, 105.*

Saul   See Paul

Silas   A Christian who travelled with Paul on some of his missionary journeys. *Pages 298, 299.*

Simon   (also known as Simon Peter) See Peter

Solomon   The king of Israel after his father, King David. God gave Solomon great wisdom and he became very wealthy. He built the temple in Jerusalem. *Pages 108, 112-123, 162, 217.*

Stephen   The first Christian martyr. *Pages 288-290.*

Thomas   One of Jesus' disciples who doubted that Jesus had risen from the dead as he was not present when Jesus first appeared to the disciples. *Pages 191, 259, 278.*

Timothy   One of Paul's travelling companions on his missionary journeys. *Page 306.*

Uriah   The husband of Bathsheba, who was sent to a certain death by King David. *Pages 106, 107.*

Xerxes   The king of Persia who married Esther, the Jewish woman in exile in Babylon. *Pages 164, 168, 169.*

Zechariah   The husband of Elizabeth, and father of John the Baptist. *Pages 172, 173, 188.*

The stories and quotations in this book are taken from the New International Version of the Holy Bible.